W9-CSK-735

A PROUD PROFESSION

A PROUD PROFESSION

Memoirs of a
Wall Street Journal
Reporter, Editor,
and Publisher

WILLIAM F. KERBY

DOW JONES-IRWIN

Homewood, Illinois 60430

© Dow Jones-Irwin, Inc., 1981

All rights reserved. Except for brief extracts quoted for review, no part of this book may be reproduced in any form or by any means without written permission from the publisher.

ISBN 0-87094-235-2

Library of Congress Catalog Card No. 80-70438

Printed in the United States of America

1 2 3 4 5 6 7 8 9 0 K 8 7 6 5 4 3 2 1

To the late Bernard Kilgore and those
talented journalistic innovators
whose leader he was and in whose company
I was privileged to work.

Introduction

I HAVE ALWAYS believed that unless one has played a part in making history, a memoir constitutes little more than an exercise in ego massage. There is one exception: a gift for writing amusingly about interesting people.

Certainly my career did not shape history, and I have no illusions about possessing any innate ability to amuse readers.

So, what's my excuse for what follows? I have rationalized it in several ways:

I am now winding down a newspaper career which has spanned 52 years as reporter, editor, and publisher. In no way does this purport to be a history of those times. But I did have a hand in recording some momentous events on perishable newsprint. Inevitably I have met, known, and formed judgments on individuals who have made history.

My other justification is that I have played a part, sometimes modest, sometimes central, in building what has become one of America's great publishing companies, Dow Jones & Company, and in the creation of its premier publication, the present-day *Wall Street Journal*. The *Journal* has been variously characterized as "the newspaper miracle of the 20th century," the "most profitable" single newspaper property, America's "most influential" newspaper, and America's "most respected" newspaper.

It is a truism in the publishing industry that the *Journal*'s daring break with traditional methods of news handling, its once highly

unorthodox writing style, its pioneering work in publishing technology, its headlines, and even some of its advertising sales
techniques have had a profound influence on the press. And this
influence extends far beyond the borders of the United States.

Superlatives are always dangerous, usually inaccurate, but the
transformation of *The Wall Street Journal* from a money-losing
financial trade daily of 32,000 circulation into America's only
truly national newspaper, with a current daily circulation of some
1,800,000 and an authenticated readership well above 4,000,000,
is, I think, a story which should be recorded. Since I am a
survivor of the small group of brash young men who had a hand
in those journalistically exciting events I feel some obligation to
report on them. They were not the sort of events which find their
way into corporate files. They must be drawn from memory or be
lost.

The appraisals of individuals and events contained in this book
are highly personal. In no way should they be taken as reflecting
the opinions of Dow Jones & Company or its management.
Indeed, I suspect that certain views expressed herein are, in
varying degrees, at odds with those of more than one of my
former associates. It is for these reasons that I have delayed
publication of this manuscript until I was no longer affiliated with
Dow Jones.

What follows might well be described as the story of a lifetime
love affair with newspapering. If it tempts some who read it to
consider a career in journalism, I would offer them both a warn-
ing and a promise.

News work is highly addictive. It is the cocaine of crafts.

*If the smell of printer's ink raises the hair on the back of your
neck—*

*If the mounting decibels of a rotary press moving up to top
production speed cause your pulse rate to quicken and your heart
to beat a faster rhythm—*

*If you have a compulsion to share with the world anything
interesting or unusual you have come upon—*

If you know no peace until you have the real answers—

Then you are hooked. You never will be truly happy doing
anything else.

The promise:

You will be paid, and rather well paid in modern journalism, for doing what to you is fun and games.

Despite periods of drudgery, frustration, long hours, nitpicking copyreaders, demanding editors, you will never be truly bored.

You will be engaged in the only career I know of where you have no need to either ask or give favors. You can look the world in the eye and, if the occasion calls for it, tell it to go to hell. When you ask searching or embarrassing questions, you know you have a moral right, many times a legal right, to demand an answer. You are not asking to satisfy your curiosity; you are asking on behalf of the American people.

Above all, you have the satisfaction of knowing that you have devoted yourself to a career of essential public service, for a democracy can function only when there is a press free to serve an informed electorate.

William F. Kerby

Contents

1

Last of the Mohicans

DECEMBER 14, 1977, was typical of those miserable, damp winter days which are one of the less attractive features of New York City. But my company limousine was comfortably warmed against the penetrating chill, and Eddie Schamp, my driver for many years, navigated the 30-odd miles between my home in Short Hills, New Jersey, and the Dow Jones corporate head-quarters offices in lower Manhattan with effortless skill. He was careful, as always, not to repeat the exact route of the previous morning's drive, a precaution stemming from the crank threats which are a routine fact of life for today's corporate executives.

As usual, copies of the final editions of *The Wall Street Journal* and the *New York Times* were in the car. I began my morning chore of the past 40 years, checking the news content of the *Journal* against the *Times*. Such is the force of habit.

Abruptly I stopped. You old idiot, that's one of the things you don't have to do anymore.

I was en route to a Dow Jones directors meeting at which I would announce my retirement as chairman of the board, It had not been a painless decision. However, to borrow Navy termi-nology, I was over age in grade, having observed my 69th birthday in July.

Some individuals count the days until the cherished goal of retirement is feasible; others battle the approach of official senility.

For 45 years, 35 of them as a senior executive, I had been married to Dow Jones & Company and *The Wall Street Journal*. I had been a participant in the *Journal's* transformation from a money-losing financial publication into America's only truly national newspaper, whose network of regional high-technology printing plants assures timely delivery to readers throughout the continental United States.

In the period from 1940 to 1977 Dow Jones, the parent company, experienced a growth in annual gross revenues from $2 million to $317 million, while net profits increased from $69,000 to $39 million.

There is a myth, and from personal experience I can testify that it is just a myth, that a man in danger of drowning reviews his life in a few brief seconds. But I did relive the high points of a 50-year newspaper career in that 50-minute drive to the office.

My first memorable exclusive story when I was a fledgling reporter for the United Press in Washington—President Hoover's firing of Smedley Butler as Marine Corps commandant for making rude remarks about Benito Mussolini. Charles Francis Adams, secretary of the Navy, was my source.

Admiral Rosenthal's invitation to ride in a Navy dirigible, an invitation I didn't accept because I had a date with an entrancing blonde. There were no survivors to return to the Lakehurst lighter-than-air base.

Then the bonus riots in the dying days of the Hoover administration; the sniper fire which missed me; the police officer who dropped dead at my feet with a bullet in his brain; the riot gas which sent me in search of medical help at two o'clock in the morning.

The Democratic National Convention in Chicago which nominated Franklin D. Roosevelt because William Gibbs McAdoo and William Randolph Hearst hated Al Smith.

My transfer to the *Journal* and my three years as a Washington reporter for that newspaper. The exclusive the *Journal's* New York editors were afraid to print—Roosevelt's decision to devalue the dollar by manipulating the gold price. A week later the White House announced it.

My indoctrination into the inner workings of national politics as a public relations man for the American Liberty League during the Landon campaign. I get to know Al Smith, warm, human, likable; fiery "Old" Joe Pew of Sun Oil; John J. Raskob, Jouett Shouse, John W. Davis, Governor Albert C. Ritchie of Maryland, and a pride of Du Ponts.

Landon soundly thrashed by FDR and a return to newspaper work. "I don't care about the money; you'll never be happy doing anything else." This from my bride of less than a year. The *Journal's* New York copydesk, 2:00 P.M. to midnight at $60 a week. Again working under the legendary William Henry Grimes, who had moved from Washington Bureau manager to managing editor and who, some years later, would become the *Journal's* first Pulitzer Prize winner.

I become Grimes' assistant managing editor and, aided and abetted by the publisher, K. C. Hogate, make some lonely attempts to enliven page one articles. Barney Kilgore is now Washington Bureau manager. He sends notes to Grimes, applauding my efforts; launches "The Washington Wire," first of the *Journal's* now celebrated page one columns.

Then Barney broaches his great idea to Hogate—*The Wall Street Journal* is to be remade into a national newspaper, emphasizing economic news. Hogate is willing to give it a try; there is nowhere to go but up!

Kilgore becomes managing editor, Grimes editor. Grimes assigns me to Washington, but Barney wants me in New York. He reappoints me assistant managing editor and assigns me the special task of handling page one and making it "unique." Readers must find it interesting, useful, and, above all, easy to read. We must give them news articles they can't find anywhere else.

"Pick anyone you want to help you." I pick Buren McCormack.

It's 1942. Hogate is desperately ill. Grimes engineers the palace guard coup which puts Kilgore in charge of the company and makes me his successor as managing editor.

The long war years—voluntary censorship; the scoop of the century we couldn't print (the Manhattan atom bomb project); newsprint shortages, 12-hour days, and seven-day weeks. D day, a 3:00 A.M. phone call over the special hot line in my Brooklyn Heights apartment. "Expect me when you see me." That turns out to be 36 sleepless hours later.

Barney Kilgore, now president, turns over the business office to me in addition to running the news end of the company. Eventually, I become vice president, secretary, and treasurer, as well as executive editor. Barney is the sole other officer.

The *Journal* breaks through the line and the secondary, and runs for daylight and a touchdown.

The long-feeble Pacific Coast Edition is turned into a respectable replica of the New York printing. A Southwest Edition is started in Dallas. An adventurous young management, backed by a farsighted ownership, strips the company's coffers to raise $1.5 million (a huge sum to us in 1951) to buy the *Chicago Journal of Commerce.* Thus we complete the national geographic penetration of *The Wall Street Journal.*

Days of glory. Other newspapers begin to imitate our unorthodox journalistic techniques. *Journal* circulation goes up and up. The advertising rolls in. *Harper's* does a feature on "the sweet smell of success at 44 Broad Street"; *Fortune* magazine writes that the *Journal* is the "most profitable" single newspaper property. We hit the magic million mark in circulation.

Barney Kilgore is terminally ill. He retires and I become president and chief executive officer. McCormack second in command, but he is my age and not too well. I promote young Warren Phillips, brightest star in the news department, first to the job of executive editor, then to vice president and general manager. I'm approaching 60, and it's none too soon to train a line of succession.

I urge the board to endorse a policy of expansion by acquisitions. The *Journal* has become a sort of economic Frankenstein; 94 per cent of the company's profits derive from this one product, a product highly vulnerable to swings in the national economy. We must diversify and broaden our base.

We take the first steps toward acquiring Richard D. Irwin, Inc., "Tiffany" of textbook publishers. A deal with Gannett, approved by the Dow Jones board, negotiated but never accomplished due to a naive foul-up in the handling of the Gannett offering prospectus.

The directors agree with my recommendations to turn down mergers with Whitney Communications' Corinthian Broadcasting,

Dun & Bradstreet, and Fairchild Publications. All fine companies but, in my opinion, incompatible with Dow Jones' operations and its cherished institution, *The Wall Street Journal.*

Dow Jones moves into the international market, joining with the Associated Press in launching an economic news service. Result: AP–Dow Jones, which successfully challenges the ancient Reuters monopoly.

Reuters invades the American market, in turn challenging the Dow Jones News Service, and inspires antitrust charges against Dow Jones' pricing methods. A seemingly endless Federal Trade Commission investigation. Then the charges are dismissed.

My old friend and golfing opponent James H. Ottaway, Sr., and I agree on merger terms. Dow Jones will acquire Ottaway's chain of eight medium-size and smallish newspapers for roundly 1 million shares of Dow Jones stock. The market gets a bad case of jitters, and our stock tumbles with the rest. Two fine gentlemen, Jim, Sr., and his son Jim, Jr., never once mention their rapidly shrinking price.

July 1970 the merger is accomplished. The Ottaway group goes to glory; new papers are acquired; earnings double, then triple, then quadruple and rise some more. The best of all deals, good for both parties.

International ventures are expanded. We become 49 per cent owners of the *Far Eastern Economic Review,* major stockholders in another Hong Kong company, South China Morning Post, Ltd.

It's 1975, a milestone year. The long courtship of the Irwin company culminates in marriage, and we are firmly established in the textbook field. Now Dow Jones has two major depression-resistant subsidiaries. Our Quebec newsprint mill venture also looks most promising.

And in November of that year every publishing plant in the Dow Jones network becomes obsolete overnight. From a mother plant in Chicopee, Massachusetts, an earth station transmits impulses to a space satellite orbiting 22,300 miles above the Galápagos Islands. Another space station in Orlando, Florida, trains a receiving dish on the satellite, brings the signals to earth, and translates them into photographic negatives of full-size *Wall*

Street Journal pages. From these, printing plates are made. I punch a button and we go to press, a historic first.

A page takes only a few minutes to transmit; the communication cost is 1/15th that of a facsimile circuit; 17 employees (two part time) staff the full-scale Orlando printing facility, and this includes the gardener and the manager's secretary. The press is operated by remote control from a noise-free glass enclosure; a special-purpose computer handles the addressing and wrapping of newspapers.

Previous technological breakthroughs were childlike by comparison—even the computer-controlled automatic typesetting, the 1,000-word-a-minute communications channels, the sophisticated facsimile circuits.

Geography, communications, and labor costs cease to be significant factors in the location of publishing plants. Repeatedly the *Journal* opens new printing centers and cuts expenses by doing so. The cost of operating the additional plant is less than the transportation expenses eliminated.

Phillips, the brilliant young editor, has matured well as a corporate executive and is ripe for top responsibilities. In 1975 he becomes chief executive officer as well as president. I remain chairman. The succession is in good hands, a deep satisfaction.

The following year *The Asian Wall Street Journal* is launched, published in Hong Kong. Its newsroom atmosphere reminds me of exciting days on Broad Street when we were remaking the *Journal.*

———

As I climb out of the car, Eddie says: "You OK, Mr. Kerby? You seem preoccupied."

"I'm fine, Eddie. I was just thinking, thinking how lucky I've been. I've never been bored."

I could have added that all of my newspaper career I had had jobs where I could look the world in the eye and tell it to go to hell, beholden to no outside influence, no pressures to do anything but report things as they were. Perhaps the most satisfying moment of my life came when a Louis Harris poll reported that *The Wall Street Journal* was America's most trusted newspaper.

Promptly at 11:00 A.M., I convene the directors meeting in the austere boardroom at 22 Cortlandt Street. We have a full attendance, not unusual for us.

On my right sit my friends of more than 40 years, the sisters Jessie Bancroft Cox and Jane Bancroft Cook, the controlling family's representatives on the board. On my left is Warren Phillips, soon to move into my seat at the head of the table.

My eyes wander down the line of familiar faces. Laurence M. Lombard, retired and now Dow Jones' first, and only, honorary director. In his 80s but still skiing, golfing, and sailing, still in possession of the penetrating intelligence which has helped guide Dow Jones for nearly 40 years.

Then there is Roy Royster, retired editor of the *Journal* and now entered on a second career as college professor and columnist. Next, William McChesney Martin, former chairman of the Federal Reserve Board. Then the captains of industry: Paul Austin, chairman of Coca-Cola; Charles Meyer, vice president of Sears; James Q. Riordan, senior vice president of Mobil. The academic world is represented by Davis Gregg, president of American College. Then Robert Potter, general counsel and my close friend and associate since the early days when we were both launching our respective careers. Then a group of "inside" directors: Jim Ottaway, Sr., Dick Irwin, Bill Cox, Jr., and Don Macdonald.

I make my brief announcement that I am not a candidate for reelection as chairman and will retire as an active employee of the company on December 31.

Thankfully, there is no wake. The Bancroft sisters were forewarned of my intentions, but I detect a few flattering tears.

Vermont Royster, a colleague from the old days, speaks a few kind words, characterizing me as "last of the Mohicans," sole active survivor of the little band of adventurous young men who broke with journalistic tradition to become the architects of the present-day *Wall Street Journal* and the proud and prospering company whose flagship it is.

I call on Phillips to give the operating report, and the business of the company goes on its routine way.

2

Bending the Twig

ACCORDING to a usually reliable source (my father) a reporter-photographer team from the *Washington Star* was engaged in its annual summer feature story rite of frying eggs on the Capitol steps when I made my debut in life on a steamy July 28 in 1908. I arrived a trifle early and in a great hurry, nine months to the day after my parents' marriage. My mother, Helen (Hunter) Kerby, who nursed her share of superstitions, was fond of telling me that I'd "always be lucky" because I was a "child of true love."

I also arrived without benefit of medical assistance, my widowed grandmother, Ella Kerby, serving as amateur midwife. My father was off on his bicycle searching for the doctor.

I was born on T Street in the Northeast section of Washington, D.C., in a house shared by my parents, grandmother Kerby, and my father's sister, Mary, and younger brother, Robert.

One of my parents' favorite stories was that three hours after my birth my surviving grandfather, Rosser Lee Hunter (named for two Confederate generals and, needless to add, a Virginian), arrived bearing presents—an air rifle and a set of lead soldiers, a replica of the Marine Band. So confident had he been that his daughter would produce a male, he had commissioned the making of the set months prior to my arrival.

My father, Frederick Monroe Kerby, was a descendant of an old Maryland family. His first ancestor in America, one Walter Kerby, patented lands on Kent Island in Chesapeake Bay in 1654. He was a merchant shipowner and a friend and lieutenant of Lord Baltimore, hereditary proprietor of the Maryland Colony.

The grandfather after whom I was named, William Frederick Kerby, married a daughter of the Monroe family, collateral relatives of President James Monroe. My mother was a Hunter, of a family once prominent in national and Virginia state affairs.

The Kerbys, the Hunters, and the Monroes emerged from the Civil War in a state of genteel poverty. My father had what was known in those days as a "good steady position." He made a trifle over $100 a month as secretary to the curator of the Smithsonian Institution.

In 1911 my father left government service and went to work for the Scripps newspapers as a Washington correspondent, a decision which was to propel me, in turn, into a newspaper career.

During his coverage of the 1916 presidential campaign, he met Eugene Debs, the Socialist Party leader and former candidate for president. I remember him coming home after interviewing Debs, and saying: "Son, I have just talked to a saint." My father promptly joined the Socialist Party and was a dues-paying member on the day of his death.

He also became interested in the union labor movement; a bitter opponent of Samuel Gompers (whom he regarded as too cautious and too conservative) and a volunteer organizer in the first abortive effort to form a clerical workers' union. He also began writing for liberal publications under the pen name of Frederick Monroe.

Needless to say, at eight I also was an ardent Socialist.

My father also became a pacifist. He resolutely refused to permit me to join the Boy Scouts because they wore uniforms.

Our apartment was filled night after night with people I found absorbing, as well as charming, to a little boy. There were writers, labor leaders, left-leaning politicians, even a stray playwright and poet and the pioneer among regional planners and environmentalists, my father's closest friend, Benton Mckay, father of the Appalachian Trail.

With my father's assistance, I learned to read before I entered the first grade, and cut my literary eyeteeth on his collection of historical novels, written by an Englishman, G. A. Henty.

This seems an appropriate point to digress to the extent of attempting to evaluate the influence which two men and a remarkable woman had on my life and my ethical values.

One, obviously, was my father. He was a kind and generous man, highly tolerant of the frailties of his fellow men and women. He came as close to living the Christian philosophy as anyone I have ever known. Although he left the Episcopal Church and became an agnostic, he believed firmly in the Christian ethic. "I don't have to believe in the Virgin birth and the divinity of Christ to know that Jesus was an inspired leader of thought." And again: "Christ was the first Socialist; the Christian philosophy will work if we will just try it."

Although he had to leave high school after two years due to the death of his father, a building contractor, and the resulting family financial problems, he was highly literate, a skillful writer, and a self-taught student of foreign languages.

He was a man of the highest ethical standards, standards which he carried over into his work as a journalist. Despite his Socialist convictions, he was never known to slant a news story. In his words: "It is the height of dishonesty for a reporter to inject his own beliefs into a news story."

Withal, my father was neither a puritan nor a prude. An abstemious man himself ("I'm afraid of whiskey; I like it too well"), he kept a well-stocked bar for his friends. In the somewhat Bohemian circles in which he and my mother moved, many of their closest friends maintained irregular sexual arrangements. Commented my father one time when my mother lifted an eyebrow: "I prefer marriage, but I can understand those who don't."

I still remember my intense astonishment when, home from college for Christmas vacation, my father offered to raise my allowance. The condition was that I use the additional funds for sexual activities. He obviously thought I was neglecting this aspect of life. I declined, explaining that I was repelled by professionalism. He said he understood, and that was the only "sex talk" we ever had.

If the ensuing random memories of my very young life seem overly precocious, I was, I gather, indeed old for my years, basically a product of my father's upbringing. He always treated me as an equal; never talked down; solicited my views; and never, ever took any action or made any decision regarding me without patiently explaining all the reasons for it. "There is no reason why you should do anything unless you know why you are doing it."

Once, when I was eight or nine, I proudly told him I was a Socialist like he was.

"Why are you?" he asked.

"Because you are," I replied.

"That," said he, "is a very bad reason. You must try to think for yourself. Do you have any other reason?"

"Yes," I replied "because Socialists don't want little children to work." (At that time the Socialist Party was committed to passage of a child labor amendment to the Constitution.)

Said my father: "Now, that is a good reason."

On another occasion, my father, who was not above showing off his son, remarked to a friend:

"Bill is interested in geography."

"All right," said the friend. "Tell me, Bill, what is the capital of Afghanistan?"

"Kabul," I replied promptly, having just read Henty's novel on the First Afghan War, *To Herat and Kabul*.

"I'll be goddamned," said the friend.

My father beamed and rewarded me handsomely, an hour's delay in bedtime and, treat of treats despite my "delicate" stomach, two fried oysters. In those days fried oysters from the Chesapeake were the standard Washington late snack. Almost every other street corner had a fried oyster stand, and from them emanated mouth-watering aromas.

Perhaps the most revealing episode of our father-son relationship occurred not too long before my father's death. I was in my 40s; had progressed from a Washington correspondent for *The Wall Street Journal* to managing editor and then executive editor and vice president of the company which published it, Dow Jones.

"Dad, you worked hard and patiently on my up-bringing. I hope I haven't disappointed you too much."

He laughed and replied:

"Here you are, the son of an old Socialist, working for the archexponent of capitalism. The son of an agnostic, you are a High Church Episcopalian. You are a dedicated reactionary and, I'm sorry to say, something of an intellectual snob. But I think you are reasonably honest and, thank God, not a social snob. Also, you had the brains to marry a wonderful wife. No, I'm not unhappy with you."

"Dad, why did you take so much trouble with me?"

"Well," said my father, "for two reasons, one selfish. First, I love you. Second, as you know I'm an agnostic, but I do believe in my own sort of immortality. You are my immortality. That's the selfish part."

Then an afterthought, typical of my father's sense of humor: "But why can't you learn to play better golf?" (My father had carried a six handicap at the very tough Congressional Country Club in suburban Maryland.)

My second mentor was my mother's younger brother, Rosser Hunter. He and my father were my twin heroes. Ross was a romantic figure in my eyes. He never realized his ambition to attend West Point. The family's congressional friend, Champ Clark, Speaker of the House, died before the appointment could be made. But Ross did take the Army's competitive civilian tests for a commission as a second lieutenant. He was notified of his appointment while his National Guard cavalry troop was pursuing Pancho Villa in Mexico. So, overnight he shifted from company cook to a Regular Army commission, also in the cavalry.

Ross was tall, dark-complexioned ("it's the Highland Scot in me"), and strikingly handsome, a dashing figure in his cavalryman's uniform and a first-rate polo player. His favorite author was Kipling. His preferred recreation, after polo, was gambling for higher stakes than he could afford. "Gambling is no fun unless you get hurt if you lose."

Ultraconservative in his social, political, and economic views, my uncle firmly believed that his heritage had bestowed on him certain duties and obligations as well as, obviously, certain privileges. In short, he had been born a Virginia gentleman (albeit an impoverished one) and he intended to live and die as one.

He was made for the old Regular Army, and he loved every minute of his service.

Ross and my father disagreed on almost every possible count, but were enormously fond of each other. In retrospect, I am sure that my uncle deliberately set himself to the task of attempting to counter what he regarded as my father's well-meaning but mis-guided views, insofar as they influenced me.

Ross would tell me stories of Hunters who had fought in the Revolutionary War and all the wars in between, including, of course, the Civil War. One of his great-uncles, an unrecon-structed Confederate, had followed the path of a number of Southern officers and gone south to fight for the Emperor Max-imilian of Mexico. He was never heard from again. He was one of Ross's heroes. "At least he didn't surrender," said my uncle.

He talked of patriotism, loyalty, honor, and duty. They were things any gentleman took seriously, along with always keeping your word, respect for ladies (but God forbid they should ever get the vote), and the obligation to be kind and considerate to the weak and "inferior."

Seriously wounded at the time of the Battle of the Bulge during World War II, he wrote me a note which I preserved. In part it read:

"If by any chance Nan Nan [his pet name for his mother] reads that I received the Purple Heart, explain to her that it was a minor accident. Between you and me, I was stabbed by a nervous French general trying to pin some kind of a medal on me. The French are always giving medals."

In truth, Bradley's staff headquarters in a Belgian hotel had been hit by a German buzz bomb. My uncle was just leaving when the missile exploded, and he was riddled with shards of

plate glass from the lobby window. In after years, he was repeatedly hospitalized as more pieces of glass worked their way
through his system.

Ross retired a few years after the war ended. His last appointment was as deputy inspector general of the U.S. Army.

He died just about a year after my father. He left the home he
lived in; scores of military decorations; and, fortunately for my
aunt, a valuable collection of U.S. stamps. Even his pension
stopped the day of his death.

But he was a fortunate man. He had lived the life he wished to
live in the way he wished to live it.

I come now to a woman whom I earlier characterized as very
remarkable. She was my great-aunt, Mary Columbia Monroe, a
spinster all her life ("I never met a man with a name as good as
Monroe"). She was the matriarch of the family.

I was enormously fond, and proud, of this handsome little old
lady. She was always the oldest of the people I knew, but one of
the liveliest. She lived in unblemished health well into her 90s.

Her mother died early in the Civil War. Her father, Townley
Monroe, and her three elder brothers were off fighting for the
Confederacy. This left "Lummie," as the family called her, as the
head of her family at the age of 12. She looked after the Monroe
place, the slaves, three younger sisters, and her baby brother.

When her father died soon after the end of the war, Lummie
sold the family place and moved her brood to Washington, where
she rented a large house on A Street in Southeast Washington,
just south of the Capitol, and opened a boardinghouse for government employees. Former Monroe slaves followed her to the city
and violently overstaffed her new establishment.

"I couldn't turn them away; I had a duty to look after them."

One, "Martha Washington," a contemporary of my great-aunt,
helped look after me when I was very small. Once, walking to
the grocery store with her, I tried to take her hand.

"No, Mister Bill. No! No! It's not fittin'. Now you walk a little
in front of me, and I will be right behind you."

Martha was as much a product of her environment as my Aunt Lummie.

Martha had only one failing in Aunt Lummie's eyes. Unless constantly policed, she would paddle around the house in her bare feet.

Lummie's own bedroom was a tiny little chamber on the top floor of her enormous brick house. (The better rooms were reserved for paying guests.) It was furnished with an iron single bed, a dresser, and a large Confederate battle flag. This hung on the wall at the foot of her bed "so it's the last thing I see at night and the first thing in the morning."

Lummie had raised and cared for two generations of her family, first her younger sisters and brother and then, when my grandfather Kerby died and financial disaster struck, she took in her sister, my father, and his brother and sister. She housed, clothed, and fed them to the best of her meager financial abilities.

When I first became aware of Aunt Lummie, things were more relaxed financially. My father was earning a comfortable salary and was able to make a regular contribution. So, although she persisted for a while in running her rooming house, she was relaxed and enjoying life.

I used to visit her every Saturday. It was one of the highlights of my early childhood in Washington. I loved her old house with the wooden shutters closed to keep out the hot summer sun; I loved it in winter with the coal-burning stoves (Latrobes) warming her living room.

Like my Uncle Ross, she would tell me long stories of her relatives—of her many cousins, including the presidential Monroes and Dr. Mudd, who made the mistake of setting John Wilkes Booth's leg; of her brothers who died in a Northern prison camp; of a relative who died with Custer at the Battle of the Little Big Horn. She always referred to General Sherman as "that evil man," and her hero was Stonewall Jackson, "a gentleman and a military genius."

It was Lummie who gave me my first drink, when I was a freshman in college.

"Do you drink whiskey, Bill?" I said no, I had never had a drink.

"That's your father's mistake. A gentleman should learn to use whiskey. Now go to the cabinet in the dining room and bring me the bottle and two glasses."

I found a bottle of bourbon (her family doctor kept her supplied with prescription whiskey all during prohibition) and two shot glasses. My great-aunt poured two small drinks.

"Now sip it," said she, and proceeded to set me an example.

Later that same spring vacation she inquired as to my smoking habits.

Here again I confessed that I had never smoked.

She handed me a dime and sent me to the corner drugstore to buy a "good cigar." "A gentleman should learn to smoke and do it properly. You will find it very comforting after a meal."

To Aunt Lummie, as to my Uncle Ross, vulgarity was the cardinal sin. Lummie used the term *common*.

One of the things that was "common" was any appearance of an undue interest in money. A lady or a gentleman never mentioned the price of anything; indeed, never spoke of money at all. Certain words were barred, such as *nigger*. "Only white trash use such words." Incidentally, while bourbon and rye whiskey were quite acceptable, only "white trash" drank gin.

My Aunt Lummie was a devout High Church Episcopalian and regularly went to confession at nearby Christ Church as well as to services on Sunday. My parents at that time never attended church, but now and again I'd escort my great-aunt.

My agnostic father never raised any objection. All he ever said was: "Religion is a highly personal thing. Go to church if you wish, but I hope you won't make a final commitment until you are old enough to think things through."

At age 20 I affiliated with the Episcopal Church, but I never was confirmed, perhaps a reflection of the contradictory influences of my father and my great-aunt.

My great-aunt, who lived through a lot of history from the Civil War to the Korean War, from the presidency of James Buchanan to that of Harry Truman, died in 1952. There was an unresolved family dispute as to her exact age, somewhere between 96 and 99.

I received a call in New York from her doctor, advising that she was failing rapidly. I went to Washington that day and visited my great-aunt for the last time. She was perfectly lucid; relaxed and comforted by her religious faith.

We had a long talk, principally about my wife, Fanny, and our two small daughters, her great-grand nieces.

Finally and abruptly she shifted topics to say: "Bill, you have always been curious about why I was so bitter about the Civil War. I think now you are old enough to hear the story."

Then she told me how, when she was a little girl, but still trying to farm the Monroe land and take care of her younger sisters and brother, the old house had been requisitioned by the Union Army and turned into a brothel for officers. Prostitutes imported from Baltimore were housed there.

She and the little ones inhabited the top floor.

She concluded her story: "That was not a thing to do to a lady."

Not one word of complaint about the years of financial struggle which followed the Civil War.

"Now kiss me," she said. "I think I'll take a little nap."

Two days later she died in her sleep.

3

Growing Up in a Newspaper Family

IN 1916 my father was transferred by the Scripps newspapers from Washington to New York City. He was appointed manager of the news bureau maintained there by the Newspaper Enterprise Association, the Scripps feature service.

My father's work, combined with my parents' naturally gregarious natures, turned our apartment into a minisalon. Visitors I will remember included Carl Sandburg, the poet and historian of Lincoln; Margaret McBride, the concert pianist; assorted artists, including the futurist painter, Brodsky; Morris Hillquit, the Socialist leader and perennial political candidate.

Of course, there were numerous newspapermen then prominent, including Oliver J. Gingold of *The Wall Street Journal*; J. Herbert Duckworth, the first American correspondent to penetrate Russia after the Revolution; Mary Boyle O'Reilly, handsome and hot-tempered daughter of the Irish patriot and poet; John O'Higgins, who had started out covering Pancho Villa's revolution in Mexico and wound up a convert and a member of Villa's elite bodyguard. Later, when the tide of Russian czarist refugees hit New York, there were added a plethora of charming and dead-broke aristocrats. They inculcated my parents in the pleasures of Russian cigarettes and steaming green tea in long glasses sweetened with jam. My father also "loaned" them money; some of which, astonishingly, was repaid years later.

I have two physical souvenirs of this period. One is a book given me on my tenth birthday by Mary Boyle O'Reilly and inscribed "To Bill in the hopes he grows more and more like his mother." (She was furious with my father at the moment because he had "ruined" one of her columns by editing it.) The other is a large and flawed old-mine diamond, which my father purchased from an impecunious Russian princess who preferred this method of financing to one of his interest-free "loans."

Strange company for a dedicated Socialist? Not by my father's lights. He hated Communists and all their works. He remained a convinced, albeit somewhat academic, Marxist, but he was also a true social democrat, who believed in popular elections and change only by the will of the majority. Perhaps even more important, he also instinctively sided with any underdog.

In 1919 my father was offered his choice of an assignment to London or appointment as associate editor of the NEA Service. To my disappointment, he opted for the latter, and we moved to Cleveland, then headquarters of the Scripps newspapers.

It was during our stay in Cleveland that the great schism broke out in the Scripps organization. E. W. Scripps, the founder, quarreled violently with his eldest son, James. James took over a number of Western Scripps newspapers, and E. W. vowed he would replace them "twice over." My father had close friends in both warring camps and was offered jobs by both sides. He felt his loyalties were to the "old man," and stayed with the E. W. Scripps organization.

Soon thereafter, Scripps, as part of its new expansionist policy, decided to start a feature service headquartered in Washington, D.C. My father accepted an offer of the job of editor, and we moved back to my birthplace.

As was standard Scripps practice, a business manager was appointed with coequal authority. The business manager turned out to be a former Scripps editor and a onetime superior of my father's, Samuel Hughes—"the boss" as he was always known in my family.

By this time I had firmly decided that journalism was to be my profession, and "the boss" was a gold mine of advice for an aspiring reporter-editor. Once Mr. Hughes said to me: "Bill, what's the most important story any newspaper can print?"

He then supplied his own answer: "It's the story available that day which interests and affects more of your readers than any other. More times than not, that will be a story about the weather."

Many years later, when I became managing editor of The Wall Street Journal, I applied this maxim to the Journal's audience. I named it "the greatest common denominator news story." My theory was that the most successful articles are those which directly affect the personal lives of readers. Continuing professional surveys fully substantiate this theory of news emphasis. Some examples of better-read Journal stories have been those dealing with the common cold; shaving successfully; how to find and keep a good secretary; how to save on taxes without cheating; companies with minimal labor problems; tips on buying insurance, and when not to buy it; and forecasts of price changes, new products, and the like. During World War II, the Journal for the first time began to attract a substantial readership among women, with the initial appeal based very largely on news articles forecasting various shortages and the potential rationing of consumer goods.

I entered Washington's Central High School at the standard age of 14. My career there was distinguished largely by my discovery that I had fully inherited my mother's remarkable photographic memory. She was much in demand by women's clubs and the like to give poetry recitals. It was her custom to read over a group of poems just before going to bed; the next day she could recite them without error. I found that I could read my history, or Latin, or whatnot assignment and repeat it perfectly the following day. This obviously resulted in minimal time devoted to study and a maximum available for playing bridge and reading what I wanted to read.

During my high school years I read, among many other books, Dickens complete; Wilkie Collins; my father's set of The Historians' History of the World, a gigantic 15-volume compendium; some of Karl Marx's Das Kapital, but not much; Boccaccio ("Let him alone, Helen; there's no better way to discover sex"); Richard Harding Davis (which helped solidify my ambition to be a newspaperman); E. W. Hornung; Rudyard Kipling; Shaw's plays; every Conan Doyle story published. Also lots of poetry, including Carl Sandburg, my father's old friend from New York days.

My sole extracurricular triumph was making the debate team.

In due course, I graduated "with honors," applied to and was accepted, on "certification," by the University of Virginia.

Some weeks later, my father attended a meeting of Scripps-Howard editors and returned to Washington convinced I should attend the University of Michigan. One of his fellow editors had recently returned from a college recruiting expedition and had been greatly impressed by Michigan and particularly its School of Journalism.

Also, explained my father, he thought it a bad idea to go to college in the same area in which I had lived most of my life.

I told him I was agreeable, provided I could be "certified" to Michigan and not take entrance examinations. It developed Michigan would agree to take me on those terms.

That summer I went looking for my first job. I obtained one, dispensing orange drink between the hours of 8:00 P.M. and 4:00 A.M. My place of employment was located at the corner of New York Avenue and 14th Street, in the heart of the Washington business section. Washington was not a nightlife city in those days; once the theater crowd had started for home, the principal business of the area was prostitution, and 14th and New York was the hub of this activity. The orange drink emporium was unofficial headquarters.

After a few weeks I probably had as widespread an acquaintance with the girls as most of the men on the vice squad. By and large, I found them amiable, friendly, and pretty good company in the lonesome early morning hours.

Being well read on the subject of sex-related diseases, I carefully segregated their orange drink glasses and put them through the scalder twice. I also tactfully sidestepped well-meant offers of free after-hours service.

After a few weeks of orange juice dispensing, a summer job as a junior reporter became available (through my father's good offices) on the then very new Scripps tabloid, the *Washington Daily News*. I resigned from my orange juice job, although my supervisor told me there was "no future" in working for a newspaper and eventually I would be in line for a position with him as a branch manager.

Perhaps my mother was correct in her prediction that I'd "always be lucky," because throughout my reporting career I repeatedly had the good fortune to be in the right place at the right time. In my debut on the *News* this happened twice in as many days.

Early in the morning of July 5, 1926, I set out to report for my first day's work. Walking up Pennsylvania Avenue, I saw smoke pouring out of a Chinese restaurant. In a moment, scantily clad Chinese began jumping out of windows; obviously the help slept on the premises.

I ran to a phone booth and called the *News* city desk. A reporter and photographer would be on the way, and "come on in." I did, and wrote my first professional story, an "eyewitness" feature. It ran with the news story and photographs of the fire. The editor, Lowell Mellett, praised me for "alertness" and for keeping my story short.

The next day I was sent out with a photographer to do a feature on whether nurses should be allowed to bob their hair. This was a burning issue in Washington-area hospitals in 1926. Driving out Georgia Avenue en route to a suburban hospital, I saw an ambulance and a police car in front of a utility substation. I stopped and discovered that a worker had been electrocuted. I phoned in a brief story and went on in pursuit of bob-haired nurses, preferably pretty ones, as per my instructions.

My feature on bobbed hair turned out to be an unmitigated disaster. My notes identifying individuals in the group pictures were inadequate and confused, and so were the picture captions. However, I was praised for my "enterprise" on the electrocuted worker, and that story appeared on page one. So I was forgiven my picture transgressions.

Shortly after, I was given the most undesirable regular assignment on the paper, writing a column of marketing hints for housewives. For this task I arose at 4:30 A.M., six mornings a week, and proceeded to the old Center Market to price produce. I then wrote my column about the day's "best buys" under, as I recall, the name of Mary Ellen. I also was given charge of the photograph "morgue," i.e., files.

My big moment each day was producing an intriguing news-related picture for page one, a photo which the managing editor thought would bolster newsstand sales.

I scored two spectacular triumphs in this phase of my career.

One morning the wires flashed the word that Gertrude Ederle had become the first woman to swim the English Channel. Up to then no one had heard of Gertrude Ederle, and there were no pictures of her available anywhere close enough to Washington to do any good. I phoned the sister Scripps papers in Baltimore and Norfolk, Virginia. No pictures.

I then ransacked our files, looking for pictures of a buxom woman swimming. Out of nowhere came help. For no good reason, someone had filed a set of photos designed to illustrate an unused feature series on learning to swim. One picture showed a woman doing the crawl stroke, and mercifully, for my purposes, her face was turned from the camera and only her ample bottom was above water.

I carried this in triumph to the managing editor, and it appeared, three columns wide, on page one under the caption:

"Gertrude Ederle photographed in training."

Then a New York theatrical producer attained nationwide notoriety by staging a party at which the feature attraction was a nude model disporting herself in a fountain, splashing champagne. A picture was essential. An unused feature fashion series yielded pay dirt. Here was the same model, posing in very scanty undergarments. It was ideal; one column wide but four inches deep. My "champagne-bath girl" appeared on page one of the *News* time after time.

Such enterprise obviously qualified me for promotion. I was assigned additional duties as relief police reporter, transferring my journalistic talents from the city room to police headquarters on a 5:00–9:00 P.M. shift. Incidentally, I ceased to write the shopping hints column. Even the most poverty-stricken Scripps paper boggled at a 5:00 A.M. to 9:00 P.M. workday.

The *Daily News*, in its early days, was housed in an ancient and ramshackle building on New York Avenue, not far from my orange drink stand. In summer the building was unbearably hot.

As I discovered much later when I worked for the United Press after graduation from Michigan, it was also unbearably cold in winter. The *News* and the Washington Bureau of the Scripps-owned United Press shared adjacent quarters. Actually, two old buildings had been joined, but the floor levels didn't match. So it paid to watch where you were going. If you didn't you were apt to be brained or to fall on your face.

The *News*, now vanished by merger with the *Washington Star*, had its share of distinguished alumni, and more than its full share of characters.

The drama critic was Leonard Hall, who later moved to New York to become critic for the *New York Telegram*. At the *News*, he was housed on a small balcony above the city room. An iron-railed staircase provided access.

Hall's method of delivering his copy to the city desk was spectacular and even somewhat dangerous. As his deadline neared, he would lean over the balcony and shout to me: "Son, station my vehicle."

That was my signal to place an empty, wheeled typewriter stand at the foot of the stair railing. Copy in teeth, Hall would slide down the railing, land on the typewriter stand, and, with the acquired momentum, arrive in triumph at the copydesk riding his vehicle. This is what he aimed to do. More often than not, he would miss connections, or the rickety typewriter stand would overturn. "Oh, well, better luck tomorrow."

Ernie Pyle, who went on to glory as a nationally syndicated columnist, was a reporter on the *News* in its early days. Ernie was just about the kindliest, most unassuming, person I ever met. And always one hell of a good reporter. He could write like a man inspired. His firsthand account in the *News* of crash-landing in a commercial plane is still one of the most graphic stories I have ever read.

His one superstition was his battered, gray felt hat. To the best of my knowledge, he wore that hat, winter and summer, on every assignment he covered for many, many years. Perhaps it would have served him better than the steel helmet he was wearing when he was killed during World War II.

I thought being a police reporter was the acme of newspapering. It was action, excitement, and, even though Washington was a quiet, law-abiding town in those days, there was no lack of things to write about. It was a far cry from my marketing tips for housewives.

I learned a lot of things. For example, murderers could be nice individuals. Like most young people, I had always thought and judged in terms of black and white, good people and bad people. I learned to think in terms of gray.

One of my interviews was conducted in the hospital room of a young Texas cowboy who somehow had strayed to Washington; gotten drunk in a speakeasy; and shot a man with whom he had a fight. A policeman rushed in and in turn shot the young Texan.

"I guess I'm going to die," he said, "and I guess, deserve to. But print this one thing, pal: I could have shot that policeman easy as not, and I didn't."

He died the next day, and the *News* did print what he had said, just as he said it.

I got into trouble twice as a police reporter. I was alone in the pressroom one night, and the phone rang. I answered, and a voice I didn't recognize said: "We raid Goldie's in 30 minutes."

I didn't know Goldie from Adam's off ox, so I did nothing. It was, of course, a speakeasy much patronized by newspapermen, and I was in the doghouse for a while.

My second visit to the doghouse resulted from my deciding that some of the so-called incidentals, unexpurgated original reports written by members of the police force, were hilariously funny. So I wrote a feature story, largely composed of direct quotations.

No less than a full captain arrived in the pressroom with fire in his eye to rebuke me for "holding the force up to ridicule." But this blew over too. When I went back to the same assignment the following summer vacation, I was welcomed as a long-lost friend.

4

A Love Affair with Education

THAT September, my mother and father drove me and a friend, who was also entering Michigan, to Ann Arbor.

Michigan had only one dormitory for men and no space there for freshmen. The dean's office did, however, have a list of "approved" rooming and boarding places. So we set out to make the rounds.

The first stop was a brief one. The rooming house owner was most hospitable and introduced us to her three red-haired daughters, twins of 17 or 18 and an older girl who looked to be in her 20s. "I'm sure," said she, "my girls will make the two boys feel quite comfortable and right at home."

My mother made some excuse and a quick exit.

"That's no place for you two!"

The next stop met with my mother's full approval.

To the day of her death, she never knew she had rented us quarters in a house whose owner augmented her income by entertaining paying men friends, and my Washington roommate and I were among the few roomers who were not sexual deviates. The place was notorious all over the Ann Arbor campus.

Whoever approved rooming houses for the dean of men must have been deaf, dumb, and blind.

Eventually I was pledged to a fraternity, and moved as rapidly as I could. My roommate, meanwhile, had found engineering not to his liking and departed.

When I entered Michigan, the president was Dr. Clarence Cook Little, a distinguished scientist and scholar, and a devotee of the British university system.

As a result, the university had a very free elective system. Attendance-taking was frowned on ("If students aren't mature enough to attend classes without compulsion, they don't belong here"); a heavy stress was placed on lecture courses; and there was minimal classroom work. Also, all incoming freshmen were given aptitude tests and, if qualified, placed in advanced courses.

All of this created an appealing atmosphere. I wound up in advanced rhetoric (the university divided its writing and its literature courses), advanced history (English), a geography course (without having to take the basic one), and third-year Spanish. My rhetoric professor had a side interest, "American regional speech." He was fascinated by my Maryland accent, which he preserved for posterity on phonograph records. I must have read one poem a dozen times, something about "Break, break, oh sea, on thy cold gray rocks."

I enjoyed every minute of every lecture and class; all my instructors were of professorial rank.

Michigan, then as now, possessed one of the great American libraries. I read endlessly.

I also capitalized to the full on my God-given total recall. I found taking elaborate lecture notes only confused things. If I listened intently, I made out much better.

It was in my freshman year that I had the exciting intellectual experience of discovering Lafcadio Hearn, the half-blind American newspaper reporter who turned essayist and poet, then emigrated to Japan, married a Japanese woman, and became a literary demigod to the Japanese.

A side note: On November 30, 1941, I noticed a small item in the *New York Times Book Review* section reporting that a limited edition, in English, of Hearn's Japanese-era poems had been published in Tokyo. I immediately wrote out a check and ordered the five volumes. Three months after Pearl Harbor they were delivered to my Brooklyn home, having been dispatched by way of Switzerland! They are prized items in my library.

Hearn was responsible for my writing a great deal of bad poetry, and short stories that weren't much better.

I returned to Ann Arbor for my sophomore year at Michigan and was initiated into Phi Kappa Tau fraternity.

Tau chapter was an amalgam of the diverse types who attend a great university. Its members, although predominantly sons of business and professional men, included a young Danish baron who was studying engineering; the son of a Detroit auto magnate who drove around in a cream-colored Stutz Bearcat; a Kentucky hillbilly type, working his way through college washing dishes; the son of the Coast Guard commandant on the Great Lakes and his roommate, the son of Michigan's most successful bootlegger (a highly valued brother who arrived after each vacation with a trunkfull of uncut, honest Scotch whiskey). In quiet defiance of the then existing fraternity regulations, the members included Protestants, Catholics, and Jews, all highly congenial. In this regard Tau was unique, at least among Michigan fraternities and sororities in the late 1920s.

My sophomore year also was memorable for some lasting friendships that I made among the faculty, notably Professor James Pollock of the Political Science Department, and Professor Walters of the Rhetoric Department.

Dr. Pollock was much in demand as a consultant. He drafted the first federal corrupt practices act and was a specialist in the mechanics of modern government. In my senior year he appointed me a student assistant in his department, and on my graduation he offered me an instructorship and the opportunity to pursue an advanced degree.

Professor Walters patiently sharpened my writing skills; introduced me to Hemingway and Dos Passos; encouraged me to try my hand at fiction, which he liked but magazine editors didn't. (Long after the fact, he confessed he had sent some of my efforts to various publications and had collected polite rejection slips for his pains.) He also was kind about my feeble attempts at poetry.

Quite a contrast with my first professor of rhetoric, a first-class teacher but short-fused and choleric. He awarded me the only C

I received in the innumerable courses I took in the Rhetoric Department. His verdict:

"You are a facile writer, but no depth, no convictions. God help me, you probably will make it your profession. Also, you probably will make money at it, but you will never write anything worthwhile. You get a C only because I don't want to spoil your college career."

I was rather flattered by his appraisal. It was the first time anyone of real competence had told me I had a chance of making it as a professional writer.

I also joined the staff of the *Michigan Daily,* the student newspaper. Student staffers were taught to operate typesetting machines, correct type, make up pages, and operate the flatbed press on which the paper was printed. All of this was in addition to reporting and copyreading.

In those years, the *Michigan Daily* prided itself on being the premier college newspaper in the United States. It was a morning paper, a member of the Associated Press, and it enjoyed a sizable circulation in the city of Ann Arbor as well as among university students. Housed in its own building, it not only paid its way but yielded a profit, a portion of which was divided among the senior student executives on the news and business side.

It was on the *Daily* that I met and became friends with Paul Kern (who was later a factor in New York City politics). I was one of his adherents in his campaign for an editorship. This was a highly political process, not unrelated to the two campus parties, which had their voting base in rival groupings of fraternities.

During my years at Michigan every national fraternity and sorority in the United States was represented on campus by a chapter. In addition, there were so-called locals, that is nonaffiliated fraternities and sororities. Independents, nonfraternity students, were in a negligible minority. Kern was an independent by choice. So he had little or no chance of a good "appointment." That year the "State Street" group swept into office at the *Daily.*

Paul Kern was relegated to editing a struggling "literary" monthly. I saw the light and went into campus politics.

A highlight of my *Michigan Daily* career was the 1928 presidential election, which pitted Herbert Hoover against Al Smith. The *Daily* had a practice of rotating news editors each day of publication. The news editor whose turn came on election night was a rabid Smith adherent. So confident was he of Smith's victory that he had a front page laid out in advance, with a huge picture of Smith (three columns wide and six inches deep) and a little half-column cut of Hoover.

By eleven o'clock that night it became obvious that Hoover had won by a landslide. "What," said I to the news editor, "do we do?"

"Leave the layout alone; I'll write the picture captions."

The *Michigan Daily* appeared the next morning with the oversize picture of Al Smith and above it this headline: "The Happy Warrior Glorious in Defeat." Under the minuscule cut of Hoover were these words: "The Winner."

A footnote to my friendship with Paul Kern: A couple of years after graduation, when I was working as a reporter in Washington for the United Press, I was assigned to the House of Representatives.

One of the rising powers in the House was an unorthadox young Republican by the name of Fiorello La Guardia. I decided it would be worthwhile to get to know him because he had put together a formidable group of liberal congressmen, a sort of third force seeking to influence legislation by swinging its voting power this way and that. I opened the door to La Guardia's outer office, and there sat his "legislative assistant," Paul Kern. It was a useful reunion for all involved. The "Little Flower" loved his publicity; I walked away from our first interview with a page one exclusive story, the first of several emanating from La Guardia's office.

5

A Taste of National News Reporting

IN June 1928, my father's friend and golfing partner William Henry Grimes, Dow Jones' Washington News Bureau manager, offered me a job as a summer trainee reporter. Then, as now, Dow Jones used this method of evaluating and recruiting potential members of its news staff.

It was on-the-job training, first working under the supervision of a senior reporter. My mentor was Alfred "Mike" Flynn, one of the finest reporters who ever operated in Washington.

Mike had begun his journalistic career as a teleprinter "puncher" in the Washington office, transmitting the Dow Jones News Service over local circuits which served customers in the Washington-Baltimore-Richmond area. Although he had had only limited formal education, a natural flair for news gathering combined with a highly engaging personality to make him an effective reporter. Everyone loved Mike.

He had his own special intelligence network in the federal agencies and departments he covered. His first advice to me: "Make friends with the private secretaries of the boss men." A few minutes later I found out what he meant.

We entered the outer office of a Federal Trade Commissioner. Mike introduced me to the gentleman's secretary. "Sweetheart," said the handsome Irishman, "I want you to meet Bill Kerby, and be nice to him. He's going to take over for me for a couple of months. Can you get us in to see the boss man?"

"Sure," said the secretary, "and if I were you, I'd ask him how that bread case is coming."

I was introduced to the commissioner. Mike asked him about a pending bakery antitrust case and walked out with an exclusive story for the Dow Jones News Service, "the ticker." Mike used the secretary's phone to dictate the story to the office.

"Thanks," said he, "and what are you doing tomorrow night?"

"Having dinner with you, I hope," replied the secretary. "That's right," said Mike. "I'll pick you up around seven."

"See," said the then unmarried Mike after we left the office. "I get a story and a hot date out of the same visit. And I get paid too."

Like the sailor with a sweetheart in every port, Mike had a secretarial friend in every government agency he covered. But Mike Flynn also had the entrée to, and the goodwill of, every official with whom he dealt. More important, they trusted him. He never broke a confidence. He never revealed a source. His news stories were models of accuracy.

Toward the end of World War II, Mike was still reporting for Dow Jones and *The Wall Street Journal* in Washington. I was then managing editor.

A sensational exclusive story came over the wires with Mike's by-line. It revealed the so-called Morgenthau Plan for treatment of a conquered Germany. In essence, this proposed that western Germany be reduced to the status of a purely agricultural area. Although the plan derived its name from the then secretary of the Treasury, Henry Morgenthau, I, along with others, believed then, and still believe, that it was devised in the Kremlin and planted on a naive Morgenthau.

In any event, Mike's story was dynamite. I called him. "Mike, I really should know about your source."

Said Mike: "All I can tell you is it comes from a man you know very well and would trust yourself."

I did trust Mike.

The rest is a footnote to history. *The Wall Street Journal* printed Mike's story under a two-column headline on page one, one of the few times that newspaper has granted such dramatic treatment to a news event. Exposure of the Morgenthau Plan, prior to the Roosevelt-Churchill summit meeting in Quebec, doomed the plan.

Many years later, reminiscing with an old friend, long since retired from the national political scene, I mentioned the Morgenthau Plan story and remarked that I didn't know the source. "Interesting," said he, and winked.

If, as I now suspect, he and Mike teamed up, the Western nations owe the two of them their highest decorations.

In September 1928 I returned to Ann Arbor for my junior year, more than ever convinced that I would never be content to do anything but newspaper work.

Henry Grimes' parting present was a pocket dictionary. "You have a job here next summer, but it would be nice if you would just learn to spell."

The summer of 1929 found me again working in the Dow Jones Washington News Bureau, filling in for vacationing reporters. For brief periods I covered every newsbeat in the executive branch, an experience capped by an ego-building three-week assignment at the White House and a parting assurance from Henry Grimes that "you have a job here when you graduate."

In my senior year at Ann Arbor I elected a number of courses in the Law School, although still enrolled in the College of Liberal Arts, an option which Michigan's flexible system then permitted. I also accepted a flattering offer from my friend Professor Pollock to become student assistant in the Political Science Department at an opulent $400 a month. In addition to grading papers, now and again I took classes for absent faculty members. I was fascinated by the law and enjoyed my taste of teaching. My father was unenthusiastic about both ventures, obviously suspicious that I might be lured away from a journalistic career. However, I assured him I had no intention of opting for either the law or an academic life.

While my classmates were scrambling for job interviews in a depression-eroded market, I relaxed, confident that I had a reporter's position nailed down with *The Wall Street Journal's* Washington News Bureau. An uncle of a fraternity brother, an executive of the *New York Herald,* volunteered an opening on the *Paris Herald.* This was indeed a glamorous opportunity. Regretfully, I declined, explaining that I was already committed.

I graduated Phi Beta Kappa, shook the hand of President Little, and discovered some hours later that he had handed me someone else's diploma.

Returning to Washington, I called Henry Grimes to advise him that his newest reporter was ready to report. It developed that Dow Jones had no jobs available and was desperately cutting expenses. *The Wall Street Journal's* advertising and circulation were rapidly disappearing in the wake of the great stock market collapse of 1929. So were the News Service customers.

So I went job hunting, scouring the market not only in Washington but in Baltimore, Norfolk, New York, and Philadelphia. The *Baltimore Evening Sun* made the sole offer, $15 a week. However, this would have involved living in Baltimore, abandoning the free room and board at my parents' home. When I explained to the managing editor that I had a long-established prejudice in favor of three meals a day, he said that he had assumed I was a "local boy" and withdrew his offer.

My friend Professor Pollock called from Ann Arbor to renew his offer of an instructorship in the Political Science Department, with a starting salary of $4,500 a year for nine months' work; more if I also opted to teach during the summer session. It was a fortune and a great temptation.

I told him I would call him the next day with my decision.

Miraculously, the next morning I received an offer of a job as a reporter for a struggling news agency, the Federated Press. The bureau chief was an old friend of my father's, Lawrence Todd. The salary, $15 a week.

It was only a few years ago, after Larry Todd's death, that his son sent me a letter, discovered among his father's papers, in which my father arranged to pay my salary if Todd would hire me. A condition: I was never to know about the deal.

Obviously, my father didn't want his son to wind up as anything but a newspaperman.

Under our arrangement the Federated Press job was temporary and I was free to continue to look for another.

A couple of months later the United Press let me know that while there still were no openings for a reporter, I could have a job as a dictation typist. I accepted on the spot. The pay was $35 a week.

Because competition was fierce and speed of news delivery life and death to a press association, reporters would phone in their stories to a "dictation boy." I would type the stories, usually a paragraph at a time, with one of the copydesk men leaning over my shoulder and grabbing the "takes" hot out of the typewriter.

In the early 1930s, the United Press had an exceptional Washington staff, including no less than three winners of the Pulitzer prize, then, as now, journalism's top award. It was a great educational experience for a tyro reporter to work with such top professionals.

Raymond Clapper was the bureau manager, and the staff included such famous journalistic names as Tom Stokes, Paul Mallon, Lyle Wilson, William Murphy, Julius Frandsen, and "Tommy" Thompson. All went on to glory in their profession except Thompson, who wound up with a lush job as vice president for the then newly formed Arabian American Oil Company, the pioneering developer of the great Saudi oil fields.

6

Reporting in Washington during Hoover Days

AFTER serving my apprenticeship on the dictation desk, I was given a reportorial beat covering the Navy Department. This was in the latter period of the Hoover administration. Charles Francis Adams was the secretary of the Navy. I have never met a finer gentleman.

With a drive on for the Navy to cut costs, Secretary Adams proposed that the needed economies be realized by closing a number of useless shore stations. The sequence of events, I recall, was that the secretary advised President Hoover of his program and thought he was assured of White House backing. But congressional pressure mounted; shore stations meant jobs in a congressman's district. Hoover repudiated the Adams program, which meant the cuts had to be made in the Navy's fighting strength. Adams first heard about the reversal from newsmen.

I went to see the secretary. "Mr. Adams, are you going to resign?"

"I'd like to," he replied, "but I can't walk out on him now. The administration is in too deep trouble."

The Navy League, a private organization advocating a U.S. sea force second to none, immediately jumped into the fray and issued a report which denounced President Hoover as "abysmally ignorant" of naval affairs. The president, again demonstrating the flair for political ineptitude which characterized his term in the White House, appointed a committee to look into the question. To no one's surprise, it quickly reported that President Hoover was not ignorant about naval matters.

Talbot, the famous Scripps-Howard cartoonist, celebrated this verdict with one of his prizewinning efforts, a drawing of a courtroom scene. The judge and both attorneys were caricatures of President Hoover, and 12 little Hoovers sat in the jury box. All were shouting in unison: "NOT GUILTY."

It was from Secretary Adams that I got the word that General Smedley Butler, the short-fused and outspoken Marine Corps commandant, had been dismissed by the White House for making disparaging remarks about Italian dictator Benito Mussolini. I scored a 20-minute beat over the Associated Press and an even bigger one over Hearst's lightly regarded International News Service.

I was making $40 a week. I was given a $5 raise, and the next week the United Press instituted a general 10 percent salary cut, the first of several during my tenure. So I wound up 50 cents to the good.

Another Navy Department friend was Assistant Secretary David Ingalls. He came from a wealthy Ohio family which early on, he told me, had become an investor in Time Inc. Dave Ingalls alerted me to the forthcoming appearance of *Fortune*, a new Time publication. It was, he said, going to cover business, finance, and the economy in a way never before attempted.

Intrigued, I became a charter subscriber and an intense admirer. I mention this episode because it had a major bearing, some ten years later, on the remaking of the editorial format of *The Wall Street Journal*. There is a literary maxim that all great writing is, in essence, a form of imitation. Perhaps the same could be said of successful editorial ideas.

At any rate, the thought occurred, as I read issue after issue of *Fortune*, that here was a formula which, adapted to daily business news reporting, could be even more successful because of the timeliness of a daily as compared with a monthly publication. After I shifted over to *The Wall Street Journal* in 1933, I would attempt news articles of this type, as time and availability of material permitted. They met with a good reception. But I remained the only producer until Barney Kilgore put me in charge of remaking the *Journal's* front-page news articles.

My UP newsbeat, meanwhile, had been greatly expanded. In addition to the Navy, I found myself responsible for the Labor Department, Red Cross, American Federation of Labor, Interior Department, Federal Power Commission, Interstate Commerce Commission, and Commerce Department. The well-heeled Associated Press had five reporters assigned to the same areas.

The geography involved was enormous. So I bought my first automobile, a model A Ford coupe. The UP didn't even pay for the gasoline.

I made my headquarters in the Navy pressroom and contracted with the public relations officers of the assorted departments and organizations for which I was responsible to call me in the event that a press announcement of any significance was impending.

However, I always made a point of being at the Interior Department around lunchtime. Interior had by far the best of all the government restaurants, and as a reporter accredited to that department. I was free to eat there, with the taxpayers footing a substantial part of my dirt-cheap, subsidized meals.

Also, I had official parking passes, so there was no difficulty with my car.

The Hoover cabinet members I knew well were a wildly contrasting and ill-assorted group. They included Adams, a charming New England aristocrat; gentle and scholarly Dr. Ray Lyman Wilbur, who had left the presidency of Stanford University to become secretary of the interior; Secretary of State Henry Stimson, known to the press as "wrong horse Harry"; and Secretary of Labor William Doak, who had battled his way to the top in union labor circles.

I attended one of Doak's early press conferences and noted with interest that his outer office was garrisoned by three hulking male "secretaries" with bulging left armpits and empty desks.

During my brief tenure as Labor Department reporter, Ray Clapper asked me if I could help out in a very pitiful case. It seemed a young Englishman had been transferred to Washington from some African post. His pregnant wife, due to deliver in days, had arrived in Canada and was trying to join him in Washington, but was having visa trouble. Could I do anything to expedite matters?

I dropped by the secretary of labor's office and asked one of the "secretaries" if perhaps the secretary might intervene. He disappeared into the inner office and returned a minute later.

"The secretary says he can have her in the country in 8 hours illegally or 24 hours legally. He says take your choice."

I opted for the legal entry.

Another visit to Clapper's office resulted in a crash course in mathematics.

"Bill," he said, "I had a call this afternoon from Dr. Stewart [Ethelbert Stewart, for many years the distinguished chief of the Bureau of Labor Statistics]. He says if you are going to cover his bureau, you really should learn something about the mechanics of statistical work. He said if I give you three days off, he'll be your teacher."

So Dr. Stewart and I labored away, actually for two full days. At that point he said I had "graduated."

If these random memories of Washington in the early 1930s give the general impression that things were more relaxed then than now, that impression is correct.

The first story I wrote for the United Press when I was assigned the Interior Department was a report on the so-called All-American Canal, now a reality but then a proposed means for transporting water from the Rockies to California.

That night, as always, my father inquired as to my day's reportorial activities. I told him about the canal story.

"My God," said he, "the first story I wrote for Scripps when they hired me in 1911 was about plans for the All-American Canal. Now you know how fast the federal government moves its wonders to perform."

Dr. Wilbur and I became good friends. I suspect my Phi Beta Kappa key was a bit of an open sesame. In any event, I had entree to his office and made a practice of dropping in after each weekly cabinet meeting. He never told me what went on, as such, but he would turn the conversation to various matters of national policy. I never wrote a news story as the result of these sessions, but I did write Ray Clapper memos which he said he found quite helpful.

During my final weeks as a naval correspondent I achieved credit for two stories I didn't write and one I did.

The Marine Corps was engaged in Nicaragua, fighting guerrillas who were attempting to overthrow the Somoza regime. At the same time they were training a native army, the National Guard. Frequent communiqués were issued in Washington. One afternoon the Marines released a cumulative listing of "casualties" covering a period of some six months. The total was well over 100.

My Associated Press competitor violated a quite common "gentleman's agreement" that standard press releases were noncompetitive. In other words, whoever happened to pick up a general release would share it with other reporters assigned to cover the Navy Department. Highly unhappy over my beat on General Butler's firing, he kept his big news to himself and flashed a story to the effect that more than 100 Marines had been killed in action.

Within minutes I had an urgent "call back"; each press association monitored the others. I explained to my agitated office that a "casualty" wasn't the same as a death and that the whole thing was a nonnews event. However, I obtained from the Marine Corps press officer a detailed breakdown of the cumulative casualties. These ranged from malaria through broken toes to auto accident injuries to minor wounds. Nobody had been killed in action. I filed an explanatory story; the AP a shamefaced correction. Everybody was happy except the AP and the Marine Corps, which demanded that the offending reporter be assigned other duties as he was "persona non grata."

The other story I didn't write was even more incredible. The Hearst papers in those days were hot after the "yellow peril," i.e., war with Japan. They had a good idea, but almost 12 years too soon.

A reporter for Hearst wandered into the Navy pressroom and picked up the daily "operations report," a routine summary of the movement and location of all naval vessels. He noted that the submarine flotilla normally stationed on base in the Philippines had departed for the Sea of Japan. What he didn't know was that these maneuvers had been a standard summer exercise for many years.

The next morning the Hearst newspapers carried his story under a banner headline proclaiming that the U.S. submarine flotilla had been stationed in a position to threaten Japanese sea communications. "Does It Mean War with Japan?" asked the headline in 56-point type.

That morning I phoned in a two-paragraph story just to keep the record straight. Later I attended Secretary of State Stimson's press conference. The Hearst reporter was there.

"Mr. Secretary," said he, "is there a word of truth in my story this morning?"

"No, Bill, not a word."

"Damn," said the reporter, "I was afraid of that."

On my last day covering the Navy Department I took a routine look at the operations report and noticed that every one of the Navy's newest class of cruisers was located at some shipyard or another. These were the so-called treaty class vessels because the great naval powers were then operating under an armament limitation treaty which, among other things, restricted the tonnage of certain classes of fighting ships. To compensate, the U.S. Navy had loaded its newest cruisers with guns.

Armed with a copy of the operations report, I descended on the appropriate admiral to find out what was going on.

So, said he in effect, I wondered when someone would catch on. My instructions are not to volunteer on this subject, but to tell the truth if I am asked.

They are all being fitted with ballast tanks. The damn things are so top-heavy with guns, and they roll so violently at sea, they couldn't hit a battleship at 50 yards.

I phoned in my exclusive story. Tommy Thompson, my cynical pal in the UP bureau, advised me the next day that orders had gone out from New York headquarters that a half-column cut of my photograph be distributed to all United Press clients for possible use on any future signed stories.

"You understand," said he, "that's a standard UP substitute for a pay raise."

He was wrong. I got another $5 raise and a promotion. Three weeks later there was another across-the-board 10 percent pay cut. So that time I wound up another net 50 cents a week to the good.

My "promotion" resulted in unquestionably the worst job I ever had as a professional newsman. I became the "lobster shift" deskman in the United Press Washington Bureau. That meant I reported for work at 8:00 P.M., six days a week, and worked until 4:00 A.M. From 10:00 P.M. on, I was the sole newsman on duty. My only assistant was a veteran telegraph operator who, fortunately for me and the United Press, knew all the tricks of the trade. I certainly didn't.

My operator friend kept me out of all sorts of trouble, taught me how to deal with the always demanding New York central news desk, and otherwise dry-nursed me through my first months in a position for which I had no training whatever.

I was all alone with my operator pal when word came over the wire from New York that Great Britain had gone off the gold standard. New York, quite naturally, was demanding a "Washington reaction" story "fastest." The UP's lone "financial expert," the reporter who covered the Treasury and the Federal Reserve Board, could not be reached; the State Department man's home phone went unanswered; so did the bureau manager's. I didn't have the private home numbers of any Treasury officials. So, with the aid of the operator, I wrote a reaction story "off the ceiling."

The only thing I had going for me in this emergency was my few months of summer work for *The Wall Street Journal*. At least I was aware there was such a thing as a foreign exchange market.

The next day New York complained that while the Washington reaction story had been produced with commendable speed, it "lacked depth" and was "barely adequate." I thought this was a rather kindly comment.

Incidentally, the next morning *The Wall Street Journal's* early edition came out with one of that newspaper's rare banner headlines and a historic typographical error. The headline: "Britain

Declares Moratorium on God." The presses were stopped to insert an *l*, but too late for some subscribers and for the *New Yorker* magazine, which declared the whole episode to be a sort of Freudian slip.

Shortly before Congress met in the fall of 1931, Ray Clapper assigned me to the House of Representatives as the junior congressional reporter. Thomas Stokes was the senior man covering the House, and Lyle Wilson had the same status in the Senate. I was supposed to fill in behind both of these star-status newsmen, but with emphasis on the House. As usual, the UP was heavily outmanned by the Associated Press and, in turn, outmanned the Hearst services, which normally had a lone reporter struggling to compete.

The UP House staff also boasted the renowned Tony Demma, copy runner par excellence. Tony in later years became the highly popular superintendent of the House Press Gallery. He also became the only individual I have ever known who could read my handwriting.

Obsessed by the need for competitive speed, congressional press association reporters developed the practice of writing a running story of either important committee hearings or important proceedings on the floors of Congress. This was done in longhand; typewriters were not permitted.

Tony would take a handwritten page or two at a time, dash for the nearest direct phone tie line to the UP Washington office, and dictate the story. He was an absolute genius at deciphering difficult and partially elliptic scrawls. They were elliptic because press association reporters in those days were familiar with Phillips code, a sort of shorthand used by telegraphers. Thus, *the* became *t*; *that*, *tt*; the Supreme Court of the United States, "Scotus"; and so on. Incidentally, Associated Press was "Rocks," and International News Service "Jits."

Tom Stokes carefully nurtured me; taught me some of the ins and outs of congressional coverage. He was a fine impromptu professor of journalism and a topflight professional. Soon, however, he was transferred to another assignment and Paul Mallon became the House "chief."

Mallon was a far different type of journalist. He couldn't have cared less about covering the day-to-day workings of Congress.

This bored him. He was a natural-born investigative reporter and concentrated on producing an occasional sensational exclusive.

If Tom Stokes had been an effective teacher, Paul Mallon provided me with ample reportorial and writing scope.

When the House rank and file rose in rare revolt against its leadership and voted down a sales tax bill, Mallon went to his typewriter to compose the "new lead" which would replace the running story I had been writing during the session.

He typed:

> lede all sales tax
> By Paul R. Mallon
> United Press Staff Correspondent
> Washington—

Said he: "Finish it for me."

And I did.

Before many months, Paul Mallon left the United Press to start his pioneering Washington gossip column, which was an instant success and much imitated. I wound up as "chief" of the House coverage, with an experienced and able reporter, Delbert Clarke, as second man, I also had a side job with Mallon, supplying more or less juicy bits of inside congressional gossip. So my net income bounded up by $15 a week. I dutifully reported my secondary enterprise to Ray Clapper, who commented: "Why not? We all have to eat."

7

Riots and Roosevelt

THE Great Depression went on and on. The White House issued optimistic statements, and the Labor Department's unemployment figures grew more and more dismal, rising to a catastrophic 24 per cent. Breadlines were an everyday sight in America's cities; so were pathetic peddlers of apples. Commonplace in the rural South were "Hoovercarts," automobiles hitched to mules by owners who couldn't afford to buy gasoline. The affluent few who could spare $25 could take their pick of the top brands of men's suits. Even though the federal payroll sheltered Washington from the worst of the depression, luxury apartments with a view of Rock Creek Park went begging at a $70-a-month rental. And this included garage and chauffeur service.

The Hoover administration sponsored two main agencies to deal with the economic emergency. One, supposed to stabilize farm prices, was put to rout by the deepening depression. The other was the Reconstruction Finance Corporation, which, under the command of that redoubtable Texan Jesse Jones, lent government funds to banks with liquidity problems and to creditworthy corporate borrowers for job-creating projects.

Even this mild intervention had its bitter opponents, including Colonel Robert McCormick, publisher of the *Chicago Tribune*.

Every RFC grant for a Western project resulted in the same stereotyped lead paragraph on the *Tribune* news story. Colonel

McCormick, according to members of that newspaper's Washington staff, wrote it personally and decreed its use. It went about like this:

"Washington—Another [insert dollar amount] of taxpayers' money went west today."

McCormick was convinced that because of President Hoover's Western orientation the West was being unduly favored in loans. He apparently was equally convinced that the RFC was a stepping-stone to socialism.

It was against this background of unrelieved economic hopelessness that, in the waning days of the Hoover administration, the veterans' lobby engineered passage of a "bonus bill" by the House of Representatives. This legislation provided for a cash payment to all veterans of World War I. It promptly ran into trouble in the more conservative and economy-minded Senate.

Thus began the great "Bonus March," a somewhat neglected episode in American history and one which brought this nation close to civil insurrection.

Jobless veterans descended on Washington by the scores, then the hundreds, then the thousands. The District of Columbia's feeble commission government appealed to the federal authorities to halt the invasion, but nothing was done.

Soon the veterans were joined by many thousands of other unemployed, and, inevitably, by "leaders" who sought to capitalize on this army of discontent. The marchers defied the Washington police and established themselves near the Capitol in a group of half-demolished structures strung along Pennsylvania Avenue and adjacent to the city's red-light district. The buildings they occupied were in process of being removed to make way for the stately complex of federal office buildings which now occupy the area. Sanitation problems, alone, were fearsome.

Soon two additional "camps" were established, the second near the railroad freight yards and a third huge one across the Potomac River in the Anacostia area. Newspaper estimates at the time varied wildly as to the number of "marchers." The consensus was that the three camps probably housed a minimum of 25,000 men, many with firearms of one sort or another. The unemployed, veterans and otherwise, combined with a sprinkling of criminals and extremist agitators to produce a highly explosive mixture.

Groups from the camps roamed Washington by day and night, defying the inadequate local police force. Crimes of violence, thefts, and robberies skyrocketed. The probability is that not one in ten was reported.

Those who, for one reason or another, were forced to travel streets in the downtown area soon learned it was the better part of valor to yield to any "marcher" demands. You made sure to have some, but not much, money in your pocket and, always, a pack of cigarettes. It was essential, on demand, to produce some money and something to smoke.

By compromise, tactfully looking the other way, and daily negotiations with march leaders, the police commissioner, a retired Army general by the name of Glassford, single-handedly managed to keep something of a lid on the latent mass violence.

Requests to mobilize the National Guard units were ignored.

On a fiercely hot July night the bonus bill was scheduled for the final Senate vote.

Understandably, senators demanded some sort of protection. The galleries had been a riotous shambles during the earlier debates, jammed with alternatively booing, shouting, and cheering bonus marchers. But efforts to get Federal action met with no response. "He [President Hoover] won't do anything," one Senate leader told me. "He won't even talk about the situation; he won't let anybody else do anything; he just sits."

At this time, an unlikely group took command. It had absolutely no legal authority. One of its members was the vice president, Charles Curtis, whose prior claim to fame had rested on the boast that he had achieved higher rank than any other American of Indian heritage. A second was Hiram Bingham, a Republican senator from Connecticut who was serving out his final term. A third, almost certainly, must have been the commandant of the Marine Corps.

Suddenly, several companies of Marines in battle dress marched up to the Capitol and fortified themselves behind sandbag barricades erected on either side of the broad marble steps of the building. They had been dispatched from their barracks in Southeast Washington.

The United Press Washington news desk deleted from my story a mention of machine guns emplaced behind the sandbags. I "could be mistaken," and anyway machine guns "sounded too alarmist."

Late that night the Senate began its roll call vote. Marchers had been admitted to the galleries, but rationed to the seating capacity. They applauded each "yea" vote and booed each "nay." The turning point, I'm convinced, came when the aged Senator Carter Glass of Virginia stood up to explain his vote.

He spoke not to the Senate but to the galleries, snarling his contempt and defiance as only he could. Neither he nor the Senate of the United States, said Glass, would be intimidated. He concluded:

I have a son who is a veteran. If he were among you, I'd disown him forever. The senator from Virginia votes NO!

The bonus lost its first round at the hands of an angry Senate. Much later it was quietly passed.

At this point, the United Press had assigned me to devote full time to coverage of the bonus march. So it was that on July 28, 1932, at about 7:00 A.M., I met with General Glassford and two other Washington police officers who were scheduled to hold one of their routine meetings with march leaders. Our little group crossed Pennsylvania Avenue and walked up to the barricade which fronted the camp.

Glassford was discussing some demand or other when there was a single shot from the crowd assembled behind the barricade. A police officer standing just to the left of Glassford dropped, apparently quite dead.

I turned to run, but a group of marchers jumped the barricade and grabbed me.

"I'm a reporter."

"Newspapers are capitalist tools," said one of my captors.

"But I work for the *Daily News*." I didn't, but it was the only Washington newspaper which had been in any way sympathetic to the marchers.

"OK, but forget what you saw. Get out."

I got out, running at top speed for the nearest telephone booth, in a cigar store across the street.

I called the UP news desk.

"Flash—Bonus marchers shoot policeman."

"Now wait a minute," said the unflappable chief of the desk, a veteran by the name of Morris (Moe) Tracy who later replaced Ray Clapper as chief of bureau. "You know, Bill, a tire blowout sounds exactly like a shot."

"I was standing beside him."

"Oh." Then, "Flash," he shouted at the teletype operator, and repeated my line.

"Now," said he, "just tell me all about it in your words."

I did, and my story moved on the UP circuits, one sentence at a time.

And so began the so-called bonus riots. They weren't riots at all, and the unfortunate policeman was the sole major casualty.

That morning the marchers remained entrenched in their camps. A scattering of Washington policemen were in the area, but carefully kept their distance.

Then came word that Regular Army troops were en route. General Douglas MacArthur, chief of staff, had triggered the long-standing emergency plan to protect the national capital against civil insurrection.

He sent for his uniform and his charger, which was stabled at nearby Fort Myer in Virginia. Reportedly he remarked that whoever commanded the force which was to disperse the bonus marchers would automatically forfeit his career.

"I won't send someone else to do this job."

Down Pennsylvania Avenue came the elite cavalry regiment from the Fort Myer garrison, horses and men both equipped with gas masks. Leading them was the chief of staff on his white mount.

Tanks surrounded the camp. The drawbridges across the Potomac were opened. By truck and train, infantry arrived from nearby points to reinforce the cavalry regiment.

A heavy barrage of riot gas was shot into the Pennsylvania Avenue encampment. Behind it went the cavalry, swinging the flat of their sabers. A second wave followed, setting torches to the huts. Not a shot was fired by the soldiers. The marchers ran in panic, pursued and herded along by the cavalrymen.

Meanwhile, thousands from the big camp across the river attempted to come to the aid of their fellows in the inner city. The open drawbridges stopped them.

There was too much going on in too many places for any one observer to provide a coherent firsthand account. So my memories of the riots are a series of unconnected vignettes.

I had teamed up with a reporter friend from the *New York Times*, a World War veteran himself. A third reporter with us was Sir Wilmot Lewis, the distinguished representative of the *Times* of London.

A cavalryman headed for us at full gallop. The *New York Times* reporter and I ran into my now favorite cigar store. But Sir Wilmot stood his ground, waving his press card with his left hand and the inevitable tightly rolled umbrella with his right.

"I say, I'm press."

Unimpressed, or unhearing, the trooper swung his saber and gave Sir Wilmot a hearty whack across his Savile Row trousers. Lewis took flight, circling a parked automobile and continuing to wave his credentials. The trooper rode in pursuit, but Lewis was too agile for him.

I opened the door of the cigar store. "Quick, run in here." He did.

"My word," said he, when he caught his breath, "who are these bloody troopers anyway?"

"They are our equivalent of the Life Guards," I replied.

He gazed at me, openmouthed, and shook his head in wonderment.

A bit later, I retrieved my car from its parking spot, and we set off for one of the Potomac bridges in pursuit of the fleeing marchers and their herders, the cavalrymen.

Our route took us down a street paralleling Pennsylvania Avenue and behind the now fiercely burning encampment. I heard a sort of whispering noise in my right ear, and then a second.

"What in hell is that?"

"Don't mind," said my war veteran friend, "it's the bullet you don't hear that's dangerous."

I jammed my foot on the gas pedal, and that ended that episode. Sir Wilmot decided he had had enough of our company and left us to find other transportation.

With periodic stops to phone our offices, we made our way to a couple of bridges; saw the routed marchers streaming across them; and then drove out to the camp near the freight yards. Troops appeared, infantry this time, and the marchers took off without incident.

I reported this to the UP news desk, and received instructions to team up with another UP reporter. He arrived, accompanied by Ernie Pyle.

It was my birthday, and my fiancée was giving a party for me. I called and explained that I "would be late," but go ahead with the party. I never did get to the party, and I wrote my last piece of copy, an eyewitness account of troops cleaning out and burning the Anacostia encampment, at 3:00 A.M. the next morning, having earlier sought out emergency treatment for a severe case of riot gas.

"Sleep late," advised a bleary-eyed chief of the news desk. "If you're in by 8:30, that will be fine."

The standard histories credit President Hoover with authorizing the use of troops. But MacArthur's employment of overwhelming force prevented what could have been a major tragedy and a bloody one to boot.

As a newly elected President Roosevelt demonstrated later, the whole episode need never have happened. When the bonus bill was again under congressional consideration, there was an attempt to organize a second march on Washington. The word went out from the White House that once was more than enough. The marchers were firmly turned back and sent home.

To my happy surprise, late one afternoon I received a call at the House Press Gallery from Ray Clapper advising that I had been assigned, among several other Washington UP reporters, to help cover the Democratic National Convention in Chicago. Typically, I was given two hours to get back to my home in suburban Maryland, pack, and make my train, an overnight one. I boarded on the dead run, found my Pullman car, and discovered that my seatmate was a quite sensational blonde who had the lower berth.

No preliminary skirmishing. "I'm your roommate for the convention. I'm helping with Governor Roosevelt's campaign. I work in your friend Jim Farley's office. I just know you are for the governor too."

Several things were amiss with this statement. I already had a roommate and was fortunate to have only one. Economical as always, the United Press had assigned its convention staff two, and sometimes three, to a hotel room. I was not a "friend" of Mr. Farley's, unless one brief interview promoted me to that status. And I certainly wasn't "for" Governor Roosevelt.

I replied as tactfully as I could that I'd be much too busy covering my first national convention to devote the proper time and attention to a roommate. But she was not easily discouraged. That night she called to me that she couldn't manage to fasten the curtain screening her berth; would I help? Churlishly I advised her to call the porter.

The next morning she was still cheerful and persistent. In what hotel was I staying? I told her the Stevens, and then went off to my room at the Palmer House.

I was assigned to cover the "stop Roosevelt" coalition; met and was completely charmed by the engaging Governor Ritchie of Maryland, one of the long-shot candidates. We formed a friendship which lasted up to the time of his death.

There were a plethora of hopefuls, because it was quite obvious that, for once, the timeworn oratorical cliché "We are met to name the next president of the United States" was the literal truth.

Alfalfa Bill Murray, governor of Oklahoma, was one of the hopefuls. I asked for an interview and he granted one, if I didn't mind talking to him in the bathroom "while I take my morning crap."

"Son, I ain't going to make it, but I'm going to do my damndest to see that that bastard from New York doesn't either. He's bad news, son. You've heard of politicians who sway with the wind. I do myself. But this one quakes like an aspen when someone says the word *breeze*."

So much for my first, and only, bathroom interview.

Not much quotable, but I did dispatch a bulletin that the Oklahoma delegation would not support Governor Roosevelt. I thought Alfalfa Bill had made that quite clear.

My favorite candidate was Newton D. Baker of Ohio, who had served in Woodrow Wilson's cabinet. The stop Roosevelt coalition seemed to more or less agree, but there was to be no stopping the governor of New York. William Gibbs McAdoo of California, harboring bitter memories of his struggle with Al Smith in the endless Madison Square Garden convention which eventually nominated John W. Davis, had his revenge.

John Nance Garner of Texas, Speaker of the House, had captured the Texas and California delegations. Under the Democratic convention rules, which then required a two-thirds majority, both big blocs were needed to assure Roosevelt's nomination. McAdoo was ready to deliver California, prodded on, according to rumor, by William Randolph Hearst, who shared his intense dislike of Al Smith and the fear that a deadlocked convention might turn to Smith.

Representative Sam Rayburn headed the Texas delegation. He consulted Garner, reportedly none too enthusiastic about the proffered quid pro quo of the vice presidential spot. But both Garner and Rayburn wished to avoid being responsible for another marathon convention. Garner released the Texas delegates. There followed a highly emotional and fiercely contended caucus. Roosevelt prevailed by a paper-thin margin and, under the unit rule, all Texas votes swung to Roosevelt.

So was a president made.

It was one of the very few national conventions which did not in the end cast a pro forma unanimous vote for the winner. Segments of the New York and Massachusetts delegations voted for Al Smith on the final ballot.

Tom Stokes wrote the UP night lead. After 46 years, I think I still can repeat it. It began:

"Chicago—Gibbering ghosts of the 1924 Madison Square Garden convention tonight named the man who in all probability will be the next President of the United States."

I went back to Washington and to covering the House of Representatives.

8

Bank Holiday and Roosevelt's 100 days

JACK Garner was something of a longtime family acquaintance. His son and my uncle Rosser Hunter had been classmates and friends in college. Jack was always extremely kind to me when I covered the House, and went out of his way to make sure I kept up with inside developments. It was through him that I first met his fellow Texan Jesse Jones, then chairman of the Reconstruction Finance Corporation. It was Speaker Garner who also introduced me to the delights of uncut bourbon straight from the bottle. No glass, no water.

Garner had a hideaway in the House wing of the Capitol. Its bookshelves were filled with half-pint bottles of bourbon. After the House adjourned for the day, I would meet him in the lobby off the chamber. "What's new, Mr. Speaker?" "Nothing much today to interest you. Let's go strike a blow for liberty."

This was his way of proposing a drink. We would adjourn to his sanctum, and he would ceremoniously open two half-pints of whiskey. One for him, one for me. His half-pint was always finished. Mine wasn't. "Mr. Speaker, I still have work to do." "OK, save it for next time."

One day I was in his office when Jesse Jones dropped by. "Son," he said, "do you have a bank account in Washington?" I replied I did and it was in the Chevy Chase Bank.

Some weeks went by, and the banks of the United States kept closing their doors with monotonous regularity.

One day I was summoned to the phone in the House Press Gallery. A female voice inquired: "Are you the Bill Kerby who is a friend of a gentleman from Houston?" I agreed. "Your friend says if he kept his money where you keep yours, he wouldn't leave it there for very long."

Several weeks earlier I had taken the precaution of leaving a blank, signed check with my mother.

I called her immediately and asked her to go to the Chevy Chase Bank, a few blocks from our home, and draw out my entire balance.

"Everything?" she asked. "Yes, every dime."

The late editions of the evening papers came out and the banner headline was "Chevy Chase Bank Won't Reopen Tomorrow."

Smugly I went about my business. About eight that night I arrived home. After some conversation, I said: "Mom, where's my money?"

"Oh, Bill, I meant to mention that earlier. I did go to the bank right away, but on my way in I looked in one of those mirrors beside the door. My hair just was a fright. So I dropped by the beauty parlor next door, and the girl said I must have a permanent. But I'll go to the bank first thing tomorrow."

Six years later I received a letter in New York, where I was then working for *The Wall Street Journal*, advising that the Chevy Chase Bank had been completely liquidated and all depositors were being paid in full, with compound interest. That check financed my wife Fanny's and my first trip to foreign ports, a fruit boat cruise to Honduras.

The Roosevelt-Hoover campaign got under way. I had one minor, somewhat frustrating, taste of campaign coverage. Roosevelt was scheduled to make a night speech in Baltimore. A prepared text had been made available in advance. The UP reporter assigned to follow the Democratic candidate was given the night off to visit his family in Washington, and I was dispatched to Baltimore to phone in a release when the candidate began speaking.

After signaling the release, I stayed on, comparing what the candidate said with the prepared text. No one else bothered; Roosevelt had an established track record of never ad-libbing. But this once he did. Near the end of his speech he launched into a bitterly sarcastic attack on the Supreme Court, implying that, when he had the power to do so, there could well be changes made. Thus, he foreshadowed his later effort at court-packing.

I phoned the UP Washington office, and was told to dictate an insert in the lead of the speech story. I did, but most of the morning newspapers had long since gone to press. The incident attracted little or no attention.

In due course, Franklin Roosevelt swept into office, carrying with him a flood of Democratic congressional candidates.

I was in New York UP headquarters on election night, assigned to writing the story on House contests. After the first hour of returns it was not a question of whether the Democrats had won big, but just how big. But the man with the really dull assignment was the unfortunate following the fortunes of the Socialist presidential candidate, Norman Thomas. The conventional preelection wisdom had been that, because of the nation's economic woes, the Socialists would be a factor in the election. They weren't. Indeed, most election districts didn't bother to report Thomas's vote that night.

Back to Washington and an assignment covering the Treasury and the Federal Reserve Board while awaiting the reconvening of Congress.

With the life of the lame duck Hoover administration measured in hours, the national banking situation went from very bad to catastrophic. Gold hoarding was epidemic; the liquid reserves of the banking system were melting away; and more than 20 governors had declared emergency banking holidays in their states.

There was considerable question as to whether the federal government had the legal power to act. Ogden Mills was then the secretary of the Treasury, a personable and accessible official with a built-in affinity for the press. Late on the afternoon of Friday, March 3, 1933, I learned "off the record" that he had been consulting members of President-elect Roosevelt's staff on the banking crisis. Furthermore, he and Assistant Secretary Ballantine would be working late that night.

I decided I had better do the same.

After dinner I returned to the Treasury and parked my model A near the exit favored by the secretary. Several hours later his limousine showed up and also parked. It was a long night, bitter cold, with the penetrating dampness peculiar to Washington in March, the kind of prespring weather which was to help bring a merciful shift in inauguration dates. A bit before 5:00 A.M. on Inauguration Day, Mills emerged. With him was a little group of overcoated figures. I recognized Ballantine. The others I didn't. Later I was to find out that they were representatives of the President-elect.

Mr. Secretary, any action on the banking situation?

My God, replied Mills, you must be frozen. Couldn't you get inside?

No, sir, but what about the banks?

They will all be closed, all of them, he replied. Mr. Roosevelt is in agreement, and we have pledges from all the governors to close all banks in their states. Governor Lehman of New York just agreed a few minutes ago.

I ran the three blocks to the United Press office, burst into the newsroom, and shouted to a dozing deskman, "I have a flash."

So what, said he, in effect. It's after 4:00 A.M., and the wires won't reopen until six.

So expired stillborn one of the better news beats.

An official announcement was delivered by Treasury messenger a half hour or so after my out-of-breath arrival.

Later that day Roosevelt was inaugurated. On Monday, March 6, he signed a formal proclamation of a federal national bank holiday. Congress quickly gave legislative sanction to this emergency, and probably quite illegal, action.

My assignment for the Roosevelt inauguration was to cover any attempted assassination. With the memory fresh of the abortive attempt on Roosevelt's life in Florida, which resulted in the death of Mayor Cermak of Chicago, precautions were extreme.

Pennsylvania Avenue, the historic route of the inaugural parade, was lined with troops, all facing toward the crowd. I, along with three other reporters who had the same chore, rode in a car directly behind the one carrying President Roosevelt. I remember remarking to the Associated Press representative that if anyone threw a bomb, the odds were it would blow us up along with the president. He agreed.

No one did. I hung around the reviewing stand until the new president retired safely into the White House; then went on home to resume the argument with my father over the merits of Mr. Roosevelt. By this time he had become an ardent supporter, to the point of abandoning his traditional protest vote for the Social- ist candidate.

I had voted for no presidential candidate. Hoover I regarded as weak and ineffectual. Roosevelt I distrusted, based in part on my dislike of Jim Farley's tactics at the Democratic convention and in part on reports from friends in the Albany press corps.

The first Roosevelt Congress convened. Those were the famed "100 days" of emergency legislation. Major bill after major bill came to Congress from the White House. Almost without excep- tion they were rubber-stamped as Congress rallied to the support of this man of action who had a plan to rescue the nation from economic collapse.

Despite early passage of drastic "economy" legislation, it soon became apparent that the program of the Roosevelt in the White House was quite different from the one espoused by the man on the election trail. All talk of a balanced budget disappeared. It was much later that the famous motto "Spend and spend; elect and elect" saw the light of print, but the theme appeared early.

The United States went off the gold standard; private owner- ship of gold became a federal offense. The National Recovery Administration was formed. So was the Agricultural Adjustment Administration. These were to be two main agencies for economic rejuvenation, along with a massive program of make-work federal projects.

A prohibition repeal amendment passed Congress early in 1933, and by December the states had ratified it.

But early in the new administration Roosevelt proposed sanctioning light wines and beer. The famous 3.2 beer was authorized, just vaguely alcoholic, but a stopgap enthusiastically accepted by an eager Congress and a thirsty populace. I discovered that the District of Columbia, often a stepchild of Congress, had been completely overlooked in all the haste.

Off I went to a congressional friend from New York, a committee chairman who was shepherding the legislation. I explained I was lobbying on behalf of Washington, D.C.

"OK," said he, "but I'm too busy right now. You write the amendment, and I'll propose it on the floor this afternoon."

So I did, and my legislative masterpiece was inscribed on the statute books.

Word of my altruistic efforts spread among my friends in the House. The next week I was the guest of honor at a dinner sponsored by a group of congressmen at the old Hamilton Hotel. Somewhat alcoholic beverages were legally served for the first time since 1917. I enjoyed the evening, but I had a nagging worry that my Methodist grandmother, an ardent prohibitionist, would read something in the newspapers.

One afternoon I wandered into the section of the House galleries reserved for newsmen as the clerk began reading the text of a bill. It was supposed to be one of those nothing sessions devoted to so-called private bills which normally are passed by unanimous consent.

I caught the words *editors and publishers*. Being a press association representative, I had the freedom of the House chamber, so I sought out a friend of mine, Representative Kleiberg of Texas.

What was this all about? He replied he didn't know and hadn't been able to get a copy of the bill. It hasn't even been printed yet, he said.

Could he arrange to see it after the Clerk finished his reading?
He would try, and report.

The bill was passed by voice vote. No one suggested the
absence of a quorum, and the House moved on to other business.

About ten minutes later, my Texas friend waved me down to
the floor.

He was excited and angry.

We have just passed a very tight official secrets act. No publication, no book, can print anything about anything the federal
executive branch does unless it has been officially released. It
provides for heavy fines and jail sentences.

He concluded: It's press censorship pure and simple, and it's
been railroaded.

I returned to the House Press Gallery; wrote my story based on
the congressman's notes; then shared it with my colleagues. This,
for certain, should not be a UP exclusive.

Within 20 minutes, a very agitated chairman of the House
Judiciary Committee, Rep. Hatton Sumners of Texas, appeared in
the press gallery.

My God, said he, my phones have been ringing off the hook
with calls from every newspaper in Texas. What can I do?

Then the story came out. He had received the draft of the
legislation from the White House. It carried the magic label
"emergency." And there had been a hush-hush explanation. So
he had rushed it through his committee in a special meeting on
the same basis and sent it to the floor for action.

As Sumners told the story, a former keyman in the State
Department's "black chamber," the agency once charged with
breaking foreign codes, had written a sequel to his recently
published best-selling memoirs. But this time, the government
believed, he had really spilled some traumatic beans, including
the fact that we had at one period read the Papacy's coded
messages to its Washington representative.

The FBI raided the offices of the publisher in Garden City,
New York, and broke up the printing plates. Now the White

House wished to legalize the action, retroactively, and prevent new efforts to print the book.

A group of three newsmen counseled the distraught chairman that he could:

1. Issue a statement, explaining that the full implications of the legislation had escaped him.

2. Personally appear before the Senate committee with jurisdiction over the bill and propose "clarifying" amendments.

To all of this he agreed. But went on to demand that we write the amendments then and there and he would rush them over to the Senate.

All three of us collaborated, but, if memory serves, Turner Catledge, later to become managing editor of the *New York Times,* was the principal draftsman. Sumners was as good as his word, and a much-watered-down version of the bill finally passed both houses.

In the spring of 1933, my former *Wall Street Journal* boss, Henry Grimes, called to say that Dow Jones was interested in giving me a job. Kenneth C. Hogate, president of Dow Jones, was coming to Washington and wished to interview me. I was feeling receptive, beat down by the competitive pressure and the long hours. And, after three years and repeated staff-wide pay cuts, my salary as "chief" of the House staff was still hovering around $45 a week.

A few days later, "Casey" came to see me at the House Press Gallery. It was my first meeting with this extraordinary individual, as distinctive in appearance as he was in intellect. A huge man, well over six feet tall and weighing close to 300 pounds, Hogate was blessed with enormous charm. He also had a quick mind, an incredible capacity for work, and a sense of humor.

We lunched at the "members restaurant." Casey's appetite matched his size. The restaurant was famous for its seafood pie, an enormous dish composed of creamed lobster, crab, oysters, shrimp, and filet of sole, topped with a baked mashed potato cover and embellished with a full two ounces of beluga caviar. I recommended the dish. Casey ordered it; finished it; and ordered a second. "Don't ever mention this to my wife; I'm a refugee from a diet."

Then:

"Bill, where were you born?"

I replied, the District of Columbia.

"That's terrible," said Hogate. "Where were you brought up?"

I replied, mostly in and around Washington.

"That's even worse! Where were you educated?"

The University of Michigan.

"Well," said he with a broad grin, "there may be some hope for you yet. The salary is $55 a week to start, and when can you start?"

Then he pulled a sheaf of my recent United Press stories from his pocket and said he had been impressed with my reporting and writing.

All the byplay about geography was to emphasize his conviction that most good newsmen came from the Middle West and, of course, the very best from Indiana. When Casey took over as managing editor of the *Journal*, he had found a predominantly Ivy League staff. He promptly set out to leaven the Eastern influence with Midwesterners. A great many were recruited from his alma mater, DePauw University at Greencastle, Indiana. So successful was he, and so good his selections, that in the 1940s and 1950s no less than five of the seven top executives of Dow Jones were graduates of DePauw and all five had attended college in the middle to late 1920s.

Kilgore, who succeeded Hogate as president of Dow Jones, was an Indianan and a DePauw graduate; so was Buren McCormack, who wound up his career as executive vice president and a director; likewise Robert Bottorff, who became vice president and general manager; Robert Feemster, the sales and merchandising genius of the reborn *Journal*; and Theodore Callis, vice president and general sales manager. Grimes, who retired as editor and a vice president, was from Ohio and had been educated at Western Reserve University. A lonely Southeasterner, I had "at least" graduated from the University of Michigan. The other prominent member of the group was Joseph J. Ackell, a self-taught engineer and the father of much of the advanced technology which made it possible to turn the *Journal* into a national newspaper. Joe never talked much about his early life, but from his accent he was a New Yorker. At any event, he was not a charter member of the DePauwites, whom, I suspect, he quietly resented.

The "DePauw dynasty" at Dow Jones was a matter of continuing discussion and spawned innumerable in-house jokes not confined to *The Wall Street Journal's* newsroom. A onetime top officer of the First National City Bank, himself a DePauw graduate, habitually greeted me as "chairman of the anti-DePauw Protective Association." When DePauw awarded me an honorary LLD degree in 1974, President William Kerstetter's citation noted that I had achieved my position despite being handicapped by lack of a DePauw education.

9

Dow Jones and the
Liberty League

THE day after my talk with Casey Hogate I told Lyle Wilson, the recently named UP Washington Bureau manager, I was resigning to take a job with Dow Jones. Lyle did what he could to persuade me to reconsider, offering a variety of assignments, including a signed Washington column. The one thing he didn't and couldn't do was offer to raise my pay. But he did engineer a letter from Earl Johnson, top news executive in New York headquarters, assuring me that anytime I wanted it I had a job with the United Press. Wilson was convinced I wouldn't like working for Dow Jones.

Ray Clapper, my first UP boss, was fond of characterizing press association reporting as the "postgraduate school of journalism." My three years on the United Press gave me invaluable background and a type of sink-or-swim training available nowhere else. It also left me with digestive problems. These continued to haunt me periodically for many years, a legacy of the intense competitive pressure inherent in the work, accentuated by being a member of a vastly undermanned staff.

Some nine or ten months before I left the UP, I came to work one morning to find a good half of the desks in the bureau office untenanted.

"Hello, fellow survivor"—my greeting from a young deskman.

It developed that a good half of the never-too-robust Washington staff had been dismissed. My friend added he would like to think talent motivated our retention, but he suspected it was dictated by the fact that both of us were making less than $50 a week. A cynical approach came naturally to depression-era newsmen.

I found the Dow Jones Washington Bureau very little changed from the close-knit, congenial group who had manned it during my summer "intern" days in 1928 and 1929.

However, there had been some concessions to the vastly increased flow of news which had to be handled in Washington. The Morse telegraph wire had been replaced by a teletype circuit, and there were two other new reporters besides me.

One of them, another of the omnipresent Hoosiers, rejoiced in the name of Perry Lincoln TeWalt. The other was a carefree North Carolinian, George Bryant, who had abandoned the study of dentistry to seek a more congenial career in journalism. TeWalt stood a hair over five feet in his shoes; Bryant had been an intercollegiate heavyweight boxing champion. This physically ill-assorted pair were kindred blithe spirits and boon companions. We became a threesome.

TeWalt's small stature, slight build, and boyish face were forever complicating his life. A recurrent problem was the refusal of bartenders and liquor store clerks to accept the fact that he was of legal age. Bryant or I had to buy his whiskey supplies for him and sneak him drinks in bars and nightclubs. After one particularly traumatic experience, TeWalt vowed, "I'm going to marry a girl six feet tall so my children won't have to put up with this kind of stuff." When he did marry, many years later, his bride was a charming, petite young lady. Their offspring tower over both of them. So much for genetics.

TeWalt's reporting assignment was the most glamorous and active of New Deal agencies, the National Recovery (Blue Eagle) Administration. TeWalt soon became close friends with General Hugh Johnson, the administrator, and the pet of his secretary, the redoubtable and earthy "Robbie." A natural gift for satiric cartooning and a Rabelaisian sense of humor helped endear TeWalt to both Johnson and his aide. One cartoon in particular cemented their relationship. General Johnson issued a decree that all public phone booths in his agency must be padlocked by early evening. TeWalt's cartoon version of the rationale for this action (quite possibly the correct one) was that the booths were

being used for sexual activities and that General Johnson thought
the time could be better spent promoting national recovery.

Bryant was assigned to the Agriculture Department and the
Agricultural Adjustment Administration (the farm counterpart of
the NRA). This was a rather sleepy newsbeat which left him
spare time to help me cover the House of Representatives.

In the 30s, Dow Jones was locked in head-to-head competition
with a rival financial news service, the New York News Bureau,
for some unexplained reason nicknamed by Dow Jones reporters
as "Tammany." A beat of as much as a quarter of a minute was
regarded as highly important, so representatives of the two
agencies resorted to all sorts of tricks and strategems.

Early in my Dow Jones career, I invented what became known
as "the whipsaw." House committee hearings always began at
10:00 A.M. At times there could be as many as three or four
newsworthy enough to merit coverage. For obvious reasons, the
"Tammany" reporter assigned to the House would dog my foot-
steps and cover whatever committee meeting I first elected to
attend. In this way he was assured of an even break on the first
news bulletin from a hearing.

It became my practice to get Bryant to cover the opening
moments of a second committee. He would phone in a brief
news story and return to Agriculture. When my competitor
phoned in his first story—at the same time I did—he would be
sternly alerted to the fact that he had been "scooped" on another
committee hearing.

The poor fellow then dashed off to catch up on that meeting
and I was free of competition for much of the rest of the morning.
In this fashion I piled up an astronomical number of beats on the
"competitive report" which was compiled each day. By mutual
agreement a "comparison room" was jointly maintained in New
York City by the two news agencies. Each timed every story
carried by the other. As far as Dow Jones was concerned, the
newest news recruit was assigned comparison room duty, and
many a journalistic star began his career in this way. One was
Vermont Royster, later to become editor of *The Wall Street
Journal*, a Pulitzer Prize winner, and senior vice president and a
director of Dow Jones.

It was during my stint as a congressional reporter for Dow Jones that my former colleague on UP House coverage, Delbert Clarke, and I achieved a fleeting moment of national fame and a couple of paragraphs in a journalism textbook.

One Saturday, Clarke, faced with the ever-recurring problem of finding something fresh to write for Sunday papers, asked if I had any ideas. The *Journal*, of course, had no Sunday edition, so I was relaxing over a game of rummy.

I had just read *Fortune* magazine's series of articles on armament manufacturers, "Merchants of Death." A naval appropriations bill was scheduled for House debate on the following Monday.

An errant thought occurred. How about a story on a move to take the profits out of war?

Fine, said he, but there's no such thing going on.

After reviewing a list of House members, we jointly decided that a first-term congressman from New Hampshire was a prime prospect. He was Representative (later Senator) Tobey. What tabbed him as a likely possibility was that he had a large Navy shipyard in his district and was untiring in his efforts to direct more business to it and, of course, divert business from private shipbuilders. This meant jobs for his constituents.

We trailed him down. He was enthusiastic. However, he really didn't know how such an amendment could be drafted and be considered "germane" to an appropriations bill. I said I'd do the drafting if he would propose the amendment on the House floor. So we made a deal.

I wrote the amendment, gave one copy to Clarke and another to Tobey. Clarke wrote a story. I didn't. It never crossed my mind that such a clumsy bit of legislation would ever be enacted. For no particular reason except that it sounded good, I set the profit limitation on government armament contracts at 10 percent.

The House of Representatives met at noon on Monday. Representative Tobey promptly offered his amendment. The chairman of the House Naval Affairs Committee appealed to the Speaker that it was "not germane." The parliamentarian overruled him, and the House adopted the amendment by a sizable majority. My whimsical brainchild survived in the Senate and was the law of the land for many years. Congressman Tobey became something of a hero and went on to a Senate seat, in part propelled by his successful efforts "to take the profit out of war."

Although I was discreet enough to never mention my role in the matter, somehow Westbrook Pegler, then a nationally syndicated columnist for Scripps-Howard, got wind of the affair and wrote a romanticized version about two intrepid and dedicated young journalists whose work in the public interest had caused the enactment of constructive legislation. It was only just, he thought, that due credit should be given to Clarke and Kerby. A year or so later, a new book on American journalism (including a section on newspaper "heroes") was published. Lo and behold, my friend and I were enshrined in that too.

In addition to the three newcomers, TeWalt, Bryant and me, the Dow Jones Washington staff in early New Deal days included the ebullient and talented Mike Flynn; Gus Tarry, a onetime Morse telegrapher turned reporter; and Oliver Lerch, a specialist in railroad news. Charles Sterner was deskman, dictation typist, and office factotum. Grimes was the bureau manager, but also the star reporter and THE Washington correspondent of *The Wall Street Journal*. Despite his repeated and heated protests to New York headquarters, any important Washington news story always carried Grimes' signature, no matter who might have reported and written it.

Although long retired, Grimes' predecessor as manager, a W. C. Fieldish character by the name of John Boyle, still retained his rolltop desk in the overcrowded office and showed up faithfully every day, including Sundays. His sole official role was custodian of the office postage stamps. These he handed out grudgingly, and only when he could be convinced that they were urgently required for business purposes.

A dedicated alcoholic, Boyle imbibed his daily quota of moonshine whiskey from a baby's nursing bottle. He had his private nipple, but, in the interests of hygiene, kept spares for his cronies. The fact that "Old Man Boyle" was not only tolerated but made to feel welcome testifies both to Henry Grimes' innate kindly disposition and to Dow Jones' renowned tolerance of eccentrics. For many years Dow Jones attracted, and kept, more than its fair share.

Among other fixations, Boyle had a deep-seated aversion to water as a beverage. This worked a minor hardship on the staff, particularly during Washington's long hot summers. It was during my first few weeks on the *Journal* that Charlie Sterner gave up the struggle and canceled the contract with the company which supplied the office with bottled water and ice. Boyle had developed a habit of launching a kick at the iron stand which held the water bottle and ice supply, as he staggered out each afternoon around 4:00 P.M. He made connections just often enough. "I hate the damn stuff!"

Boyle also envisioned himself as unofficial critic of all news stories produced by the staff, including those written by Grimes. He frowned on any departure from the exact text of an official press release. He called this "maximizing." In his mind this constituted a gross breach of good journalism. "You," he said to me one morning shortly after I had joined the staff, "are another goddamned maximizer like Grimes."

Far from being an office pest, Boyle was a source of endless anecdotes and added an element of spice, variety, and adventure. He was forever getting into trouble. All of us tried to look after him, but Sterner and Flynn were his particular nursemaids. Time after time they rescued him from the clutches of the Washington police; appeased the wrath of the National Press Club management; and made sure that he used the men's room rather than the women's room. This last was a real necessity because, when hard pressed, he failed to discriminate. Both facilities were just down the hall from our National Press Building office.

Late one afternoon, I heard feminine squeals and outraged cries in the hallway.

"Oh, God," said Sterner, jumping to his feet, "I didn't think he was that drunk."

A few minutes later he returned with John Boyle in tow. He had found him serenely completing his business in an emptied women's room.

Sterner pacified an agitated building manager, and thereafter someone always chaperoned Boyle whenever he made one of his frequent exits.

Obviously, the old man had a constitution of steel. Some three years after I moved to New York, when he was deep in his 80s, he was killed crossing 14th Street on his way home. He staggered in front of an automobile, was knocked down, but arose and staggered in front of a truck coming in the opposite direction. That did it. As Charlie Sterner remarked, "No one car could have done him in."

After his death it seemed only proper to make a perfunctory inventory of the contents of his ancient rolltop desk, which, drunk or sober, he always kept carefully locked. In a drawer were more than $100,000 in U.S. Treasury bearer bonds, with many years' accumulation of uncashed coupons. There were also a dozen or more ardent letters addressed to "Dear Mrs. Q." None had been finished, and, obviously, none had been mailed to the mysterious lady in his life.

William Henry Grimes presided over our Washington news coverage with the sure touch of a veteran first-class journalist. His early newspapering had been as a reporter for papers in his native Ohio. His first major story, he once told me, was an exposé of working conditions among itinerant farmhands. Grimes had got himself hired as a lettuce picker. He had been selected for the exposé assignment because "I looked so boyish and naive." He was not quite 20 at the time, having left Western Reserve University in Cleveland at the end of his junior year.

Grimes managed the UP Washington Bureau for a while, and was largely responsible for assembling the fine staff which I found working there when I joined the United Press. Later he organized the UP's specialized business and financial news report, When he was hired to replace John Boyle as Dow Jones Washington Bureau chief, he was producing his own syndicated news service from Washington.

If ever there was a reporter who knew where all the bodies were buried in Washington, it was Henry Grimes. Grimes had a reservoir of excellent sources, including Eugene Meyer, then chairman of the Federal Reserve Board, and Andrew Mellon when he was secretary of the Treasury. In addition to possessing great reportorial skills, Grimes could make a typewriter sing. Some years later, when editor of *The Wall Street Journal*, he became the first newsman on that publication to win a Pulitzer Prize, then, as now, the most prestigious of journalistic honors.

Like many individuals with great talent, Grimes was not without eccentricities. He read omnivorously, but never, ever, a book. "I have no patience with long-winded writing." The theater bored him, "except for the Marx Brothers." He was passionately fond of golf and bridge, and played both with a ferocious intensity.

He was renowned for his temper tantrums, but almost never were they directed at his own staff. He reserved his outbursts for the New York editors, public relations men, and what he regarded as his own failures. At golf he was a club thrower; at bridge, a card hurler. A missed putt or a mistake at the card table (his, but never a partner's) would produce an awe-inspiring burst of rage. Grimes' mortal enemy at New York headquarters was the then managing editor, a pompous misfit by the name of Cy Kissane. Grimes' nickname for him was "Stupid."

Among other annoying aberrations, Kissane was a devotee of Walter Winchell's gossip column. It was his custom to deluge the Washington Bureau with messages stating Winchell says, send story soonest.

Once Winchell gave currency to a particularly wild rumor to the effect that the president was considering resigning. Kissane demanded a story "soonest."

Charlie Sterner handed Grimes the message from the teletype. Purple-faced, Grimes rose and leveled a kick at his typewriter stand. It flew across the office, banged the wall, and the typewriter wound up on the floor, a mangled mass of wreckage.

To Sterner: "Tell Stupid to go to Hell."

To me: "Bill, please call the typewriter people and tell them I need a new machine immediately." Then, "And tell them to bill me personally."

Sterner dispatched a diplomatically censored version of the reply, and I talked the Royal dealer into dispatching a replacement machine right away.

Grimes had his own method of disciplining the New York news editors, who had an annoying habit of holding first-class exclusive stories for days and days. He allowed them exactly seven days from the date of filing. Then, if the story had not appeared in print, he would tip off one or another of his cronies working for other New York newspapers. The story would appear promptly and, almost inevitably, there would be a complaint from someone in New York that we had been scooped.

To which Grimes would reply: Look in your unused story file. You have had the same story for seven days and didn't use it. News won't hold forever.

But deep as was his contempt for the New York news editors, Grimes reserved his most profound loathing for public relations men. He regarded them as some sort of subspecies of humanity and the natural enemies of honest newsmen. When one of his longtime friends left newspaper work to accept a position as public relations man for a government agency, Grimes was deeply upset. "There must be some flaw in his character which I didn't detect over all these years."

I vividly recall one episode which occurred when the head of an advertising—public relations agency had the temerity to beard Grimes in his office in an attempt to pressure Grimes into writing a story from a bank's press release. In an excess of zeal, he reminded Grimes that his agency also handled the advertising for another, much larger financial organization which did sizable advertising in *The Wall Street Journal.*

Grimes fixed him with a baleful stare, and remarked very quietly but very distinctly: "The president of that company is a close personal friend of mine. He will be very interested to hear that you are using his advertising account to force a news story about one of his competitors."

The visitor turned pale and clutched his chest. "Oh, my heart! My heart!"

Grimes: "If you intend to die, get the hell out of my office and do it somewhere else."

The man staggered out, still clutching his chest.

Said Grimes to me: "Follow him and make sure the poor fellow isn't really sick."

I did, and was able to report a fast recovery.

But for all his crusty exterior, the real man was kindly and sentimental, and unshakably loyal to family, friends, and staff. He called me over to his apartment one December night in 1942 to tell me that Barney Kilgore was being promoted to general manager of Dow Jones and that I would succeed Kilgore as managing editor of *The Wall Street Journal*. When he told me the news, there were tears in his eyes.

I attempted a feeble joke. "Henry, I hope I won't be that much of a disaster."

He mopped his eyes and grinned. Then, "I'm just so happy my boy made it."

During my stint in the Washington Bureau, Eugene Meyer purchased the ailing and feeble *Washington Post*. His dream was to convert it into a truly national newspaper, and, although he had no background in publishing, he was astute enough to realize that the one nationwide common news denominator was business and finance. He promptly offered Grimes a top editorial position. Grimes declined and, as one of his reasons, said he didn't want to abandon his Washington staff. "Oh, that's no problem," said Meyer. "I'll hire the whole bureau and pay them more than whatever they are getting now."

Perhaps fortunately for the future of *The Wall Street Journal*, Meyer's advisers convinced him that a national newspaper was impractical, because newspaper advertising was basically local retail and timely distribution was impossible outside a very limited area. Logic appeared to be on their side, but there were solutions, as the *Journal* was to demonstrate not too many years later.

In 1934 Grimes was transferred to New York to replace his old sparring mate, Kissane, as managing editor. Typical of his softheartedness and his reluctance to hurt anyone's feelings, he left potential chaos behind him. To me he explained that while he didn't know what the final decision would be, in the meantime he would "rely" on me to run the Washington Bureau. So I assumed I was acting manager, particularly as I had filled that role during his vacations. However, a few days after Grimes departed for New York, I gave Mike Flynn an assignment. "What gives?" said the good-natured Mike. "I make the assignments around here." Comparing notes, we discovered that Mike, like me, was being "relied" on by Grimes to keep the bureau functioning. We were close friends and reached an amicable compromise. Actually, the hydra-headed office operated fairly effectively until a new manager arrived from New York.

Grimes moved fast and decisively to reorganize the New York news operation. His theme was that from now on the *Journal* would be run as a newspaper, with emphasis on news!

Operating methods which had prevailed unquestioned since the days of Dow and Jones were reformed overnight. Grimes swept sentiment aside to kill the afternoon, and original, edition of *The Wall Street Journal*. (With the securities markets in doldrums, sales of the afternoon edition, all newsstand, had shrunk to a few thousand copies.) He hired the first makeup editor in the history of the paper when he discovered that news placement was pretty much left to the discretion of the composing room foreman. His criterion was not, was a story important, but rather, did it fit neatly in a particular location. Grimes also personally supervised the destruction of many columns of "filler" type, timeless material which had been used over and over to plug awkward holes on pages.

The *Journal's* sole morning edition, pre Grimes, had been put to bed at a gentlemanly 6:00 P.M., and day after day appeared missing important news. Grimes decreed a three-edition paper, with the final going to press around 11:30 P.M.

Grimes also organized the first copydesk in the history of the *Journal*. He recruited first-class deskmen and, to the horror of the reportorial staff, gave them the authority to edit, rewrite (if necessary), and headline. Previously there had been one lone denizen of the desk who was supposed to check proofs for typographical errors and perform other mechanical chores. He didn't edit, and the reporters wrote their own headlines.

What true editing was done was performed by two overworked "news editors" who had the chore of reviewing all "special" and "important," i.e., nonroutine, news articles. This system explained in part, at least, the mysterious delays between receipt of an important Washington news story and its appearance in print.

Grimes abolished the news editor positions and, finding no spot for one of the occupants, Thomas Phelps, dispatched him to Washington as bureau manager.

Our new chief was a personable, highly intelligent, intensely literal-minded individual who continued the 12 hours per day, seven days per week schedule to which he had become accustomed in his New York job. He was violently miscast in his new role of handling a never-ending flow of swiftly developing major spot-news stories. By natural bent and training he was a securities analyst, and a good one, as he was to demonstrate when he abandoned journalism for the securities business.

But Phelps was a lost man in Washington. The operations of Congress and the Roosevelt administration baffled him. "But it's not the logical thing to do" was his plaintive and repeated complaint. He also refused to acknowledge that political expediency played a sizable role in policy decisions affecting the national economy. He was always seeking the "real reason."

By natural instinct and training Tom was a perfectionist. He would debate endlessly over the choice of an adjective and matters of minor punctuation. He drove the New York copydesk wild with messages requesting insertion of a comma after such and such a word in such and such a paragraph. He wrote slowly and meticulously; then rewrote his own copy endlessly to the point of violating deadlines. I recall dropping by the office one Friday night after the theater. It was around midnight, and there was Tom Phelps, all alone, banging away at his typewriter. The Saturday *Journal*, of course, had long since gone to press.

I asked if he was doing a piece for Monday's paper. No, said Phelps. Grimes made me file a story before I was satisfied with it. I'm sure I can do better, so I'm practicing.

Early in his Washington career, Phelps expressed a desire to meet Representative Tinkham, an influential, conservative congressman from Massachusetts. I arranged it, and we had dinner with Tinkham. Later, he took us to his apartment in the Carlton Hotel, then Washington's finest, to show off his collection of big game trophies.

In the course of the tour, Tinkham remarked that his African safaris had been greatly aided by his fluency in Swahili, a widely spoken native dialect.

Whereupon Tom Phelps delivered a long speech in a, to me, incomprehensible tongue.

"What's that gibberish?" demanded Tinkham.

"Swahili, of course," replied Phelps, truthfully if not tactfully.

That ended his efforts to establish an entente cordiale with the congressman.

On the way down in the elevator Phelps remarked:

"He's an old fraud. I'll bet he bought all those trophies."

How did Phelps learn Swahili? It developed Tom once had spent six months tramping through the African interior with an entourage of a couple of dozen natives, none of whom understood more than a few words of English.

Phelps' first staff meeting did not endear him to his reporters. He called it for a Saturday noon. By long established custom, our workday on Saturday ended at noon. But our new chief announced he was putting a stop to that slovenly practice. From now on, Saturday was just another workday. He realized government offices closed at noon, but he was sure there was news to be had anyway. "Now," he concluded, "everybody go back to work and see if each one of you can't bring me back a scoop."

TeWalt, Bryant, and I went off to see Walter Johnson pitch for the Senators against Connie Mack's Philadelphia Athletics. At the end of each inning, Bryant would turn to us and anxiously inquire if we had developed "any scoops yet."

Soon after Phelps arrival on the scene, I managed what was by far the great achievement of my life. I persuaded one Frances Douglass to agree to marry me, and we set the date for the following June, when she would graduate from George Washington University.

For the first time in my young professional career, my salary became more important than my job. Hours and hours of agonized budgeting convinced me that I must earn $70 a week to support a wife. I was making $60, the $55 salary at which I had been hired plus $5 a week for writing a Washington column for *the Boston News Bureau*, a long-deceased Dow Jones daily, then circulating in New England. For the only time in my career, I asked for a raise in pay. Phelps, quite honestly, pleaded lack of authority and referred the matter to Grimes in New York. With equal honesty, Grimes responded by saying: "No one is getting a raise."

Out of the blue came a job offer from my old friend of United Press days, William C. Murphy, Jr., who, it developed, had been engaged as public relations director for the fledgling American Liberty League. This well-heeled organization had been formed to do battle with the Roosevelt New Deal. While bipartisan, it numbered among its prominent supporters a sizable group of conservative old-line Democrats. These included Al Smith, John W. Davis, John J. Raskob, Jouett Shouse, and former Governor Ritchie of Maryland. Also prominent were several members of the Du Pont family and other industrialists, including Ernest Weir, the steel magnate.

I would be second man in the public relations department, said Murphy, and the salary would be $105 a week, an astronomical sum for the depths of the depression.

My early distrust of Franklin D. Roosevelt had hardened over the first two years of his administration into a firm conviction that he was a political opportunist leading the nation on a disaster course. Thus both Liberty League ideology and income were appealing. I could tackle my new job with enthusiasm and be handsomely paid to boot.

My Socialist father endorsed the move. "You believe in what you are doing. So go do it."

The next morning I called Murphy to accept and notified Grimes and Phelps. Grimes made a trip to Washington to tell me I was "a natural born newsman" and was "destroying my career." I held firm, and his parting comment was, "I can't fight sex."

My stint at the Liberty League contributed another segment of valuable background. Murphy concentrated on policy matters. He disliked administrative work and loathed anything having to do with fund raising. To me both these aspects of the job were new and challenging. I ran a sizable staff; wrote fund-raising pamphlets; handled the purchasing of millions of dollars worth of printing and other supplies. All of this gave me my baptism by fire in administrative work.

Even more fascinating were occasional contacts with some of my longtime heroes. The highlight was assisting Bill Murphy in arranging the historic Al Smith dinner at Washington's Mayflower Hotel. This was the stage for Smith's break with the Democratic Party of the New Deal. "As for me, I'll take a walk!"

A few weeks later I was assigned to accompany Smith to a Senate hearing. As we walked down one of the marble corridors of the Senate Office Building, we passed a bedraggled, elderly woman scrubbing away.

"Wait a minute," said Smith. "I think she's an old friend."

"Maggie, Maggie O'Riley."

The scrubwoman looked up and smiled.

"Hi, Al, How's things?"

They had attended grade school together on New York's East Side. After a lengthy reunion, Smith went on his way, with the promise, "I think I can get a better job for you."

He did.

The man wasn't running for anything. He had no audience to play to. He was just being Al Smith, a very nice and human person.

The only thing I ever found artificial about Smith was his Lower East Side accent. In ordinary conversation he spoke all but accentless English. But in public and on the campaign trail he reverted to his trademarked "thoid," and "raadio," and so on.

Obviously, the Liberty League backed Alfred Landon of Kansas in his spectacularly unsuccessful effort to defeat Roosevelt's bid for a second term. After the election it quietly disbanded, and I plunged from affluence to joblessness.

My highly embryonic talents at fund raising and public relations produced spontaneous offers in these fields, but after consulting with my bride, I determined to return to newspaper work. "You won't be happy doing anything else. Never mind the money, we'll make out."

A phone call to Grimes in New York produced an immediate offer of a job on the New York copydesk, but "your pay will be exactly what you were making when you left." My wife was standing beside me. I told her what Grimes had said. "Take it, and when do we leave for New York?"

10

The Grimes Regime

A few days before Thanksgiving of 1936, Fanny and I settled into a one-room apartment on Sheridan Square in the heart of Greenwich Village, a handy location for my new job on the *Journal*'s copydesk. Our abode had the added merit of being a brand-new building with good security, and tough-minded doormen on 24-hour duty. The first time our friend and near neighbor Perry TeWalt sought admission before I got home from work, the night man called me at the office for an OK. Fanny's word wasn't good enough!

TeWalt had been transferred from Washington to New York and assigned by Grimes to the exacting duty of writing the page one news summary, "What's News." This feature, since much imitated by other newspapers, was the brilliant journalistic invention of Casey Hogate. It rapidly became, and remains today, *The Wall Street Journal*'s best-read section, repeatedly scoring in the high 90 percents on readership surveys.

TeWalt wound up his chores around 10:30 P.M., a good hour before my duties were over. Sometimes alone, sometimes in company with other bachelors on the *Journal*'s night news staff, he would pick up Fanny at our apartment and proceed to an agreed-on meeting place. Frequently this was the bar of the old Astor Hotel on Times Square. I would join up around midnight or a bit later. We became night people in the true New York sense.

Usually we wound up our adventures around 4:00 or 5:00 A.M. at Jack Delaney's bar and restaurant, just across the street from our apartment. In addition to good food and sturdy, honest drinks (Delaney's had started life as a well-reputed speakeasy during prohibition), the establishment boasted a talented, alcoholic piano player. When sufficiently stimulated by free Scotches, he could be induced to play the difficult *Rhapsody in Blue*. Morning after morning, we crossed Sheridan Square, bed bound, with the strains of this Gershwin masterpiece singing in our heads.

When our year lease was up, we moved to Brooklyn Heights, an old and attractive residential area just across the harbor from lower Manhattan, one subway stop from the office. We were to remain in this location for more than 35 years, inhabiting a series of apartments and eventually a town house built in the 1780s.

The new apartment boasted a living room, bedroom, full kitchen, and bath, and the rent was a much-appreciated $10 per month less than that of our Greenwich Village establishment.

Fanny and I were warmly welcomed by my new colleagues in New York. One of the most hospitable was Oliver J. Gingold, even then the patriarch of the news staff, with service dating to 1910. This was the same Oliver Gingold who had been one of my father's close newspaper friends during dad's stint in New York. Oliver was a widower, and his bachelor establishment was presided over by an aged Czech woman who combined a talent for superb cookery with fanatical devotion to a clean and orderly apartment. An invitation to bridge and dinner was much prized by the *Journal's* news staffers. For me there was always cheesecake.

Despite age disparity, Oliver and Fanny and I became the closest of friends. Later, when Oliver remarried, the attractive and vivacious Maxine Gingold made it a foursome.

Oliver, although not the most facile of writers, had an incredible nose for news, and I never found a publicly owned company where he did not have a sure source. "Oliver, I hear such and such a rumor." He would check—always by phone—and his reports were never at fault.

My father, that apostle of inflexible honesty in reporting, had admiringly cited Gingold to me as an example to be emulated, a man who could, but didn't, make a personal fortune from being the first to know about news events affecting values of securities or commodities. During World War I, Oliver, English by birth, had the inside track at the British Purchasing Commission in New York. Time after time he would phone in stories to the Dow Jones

News Service which sent commodities skyrocketing. "You know," said my father, "it never even crossed his mind that he could make a little quiet money on the side by speculating in cotton or some other commodity."

One other Gingold anecdote:

Without any initiative on my part, I was notified that I had been elected to a New York newspaper organization, the Society of Silurians. A notice thanked me for my dues payment. Inquiry developed that an "anonymous friend" was responsible.

I confronted Oliver. "Well," said he, "why should I know anything about it? But I think it is a mighty fine thing that you and Fred [my father] have become the only father and son to be members of Silurians at the same time."

In very late life, Oliver suffered from a type of progressive paralysis. The first symptoms occurred when he and Maxine were our guests at our home in the Pocono Mountains of Pennsylvania. Eventually he had to be transported to and from the office in an automobile rented for that purpose and equipped with a portable wheelchair.

"Oliver Gingold," decreed Barney Kilgore, "will never be retired. He will be a member of the *Journal's* news staff until the day of his death."

Oliver died, after a brief hospitalization, on March 8, 1966, the day after he had assured me in a strong voice, "I'll be back soon." He was in his 56th year of unbroken service with Dow Jones.

Gingold's proudest boast was that he had coined the term *blue chip* to describe a high-grade stock.

His favorite anecdote was about an early managing editor of *The Wall Street Journal* who abandoned wife and family to elope with Dow Jones' then sole telephone operator. Said Oliver: "We didn't miss the managing editor at all, but it was chaos without anyone to run the switchboard."

He never did finish his memoirs, which he had titled:

"I Survived 37 Managing Editors"

Tom Phelps' tenure as Washington manager was relatively brief. Not long after I went to work for the Liberty League, he was appointed editor of Barron's magazine, a Dow Jones financial weekly, a position highly compatible with his undoubted talents. His replacement was my friend Bernard Kilgore. Barney had been writing an editorial page column at New York headquarters after a term as managing editor of the *Journal's* Pacific Coast Edition.

Kilgore rented an apartment in the same building in Washington in which Fanny and I had set up housekeeping, but only after I had agreed to "guarantee" not only his rent but his good behavior. The landlord was highly suspicious of young bachelors.

Fanny kept an eye on Kilgore's household arrangements and supplied him with dates. The latter was no particular chore. Barney was a handsome young man, a dead ringer for the then popular band leader and movie star Buddy Rogers. More than once, he was besieged by eager autograph seekers in one of Washington's nightclubs.

Barney acquired a cook and factotum and launched himself on a Washington social career, partly because he loved a party and partly to acquire useful contacts. Very quickly he became a respected and popular figure in the somewhat snobbish Washington press corps, a tribute both to his professional skills and to his attractive personality. The ultimate accolade was accorded him when he was elected a member of the Gridiron Club, the first *Journal* staff member to belong to that elite organization of Washington journalists.

Kilgore worked even harder than he played. He rebuilt the Washington Bureau's shaky morale and used his influence with Hogate to wheedle money to add to the thin staff. In common with most really gifted editors, Barney had the ability to spread his writing talent around the staff, vastly improving the product of even the most mediocre craftsman. The Washington news file had been superior under Grimes. Under Kilgore it became superb, and the *Journal's* Washington Bureau became recognized in the profession as one of the best covering the nation's capital.

Barney's prize addition to his group of reporters was Eugene Duffield, whom he lured away from the *Chicago Tribune*. Gene, a close friend of mine, came to my Liberty League office to talk over Barney's job offer. I gave Kilgore and his operations the high

marks they deserved, and Duffield called Barney from my office
to give his acceptance.

A perceptive reporter and brilliant wordsmith, Duffield was a
worthy successor to Barney as Washington manager when Kilgore
moved on to New York as managing editor. However, very soon
after Pearl Harbor, Gene took a leave of absence to serve as
Secretary James Forrestal's executive assistant. He never
returned to the *Journal*, despite every argument Kilgore and I
could muster.

"I have two reasons for not coming back," said Gene. "You,
Barney, are one. Bill is the other. I want to be top man, and I can't
do it with you two around." Eventually, he wound up as president
and publisher of a group of magazines. We remained good friends
and were neighbors in Brooklyn Heights. I have no doubt his
defection constituted the greatest single loss of journalistic talent
in my 45-plus years of service with *The Wall Street Journal*.

Because of my background, my special chore on the New York
copydesk was handling all Washington stories. This resulted in
my working closely with Kilgore. Now and again, I would forward story suggestions which he welcomed enthusiastically.

In 1938 Grimes appointed me assistant managing editor of both
the *Journal* and the Dow Jones News Service, the "ticker." Thus I
was presiding over the ticker copydesk on October 1, when
Hitler's troops entered the Sudetenland, a German-speaking area
ceded to Germany by a Czechoslovakia left helpless and stripped
of allies by the Munich agreement.

Grimes was a habitually slow starter in the morning, and it was
his custom to come to work around noon or later. However, he
had a Dow Jones News Service printer in his Brooklyn Heights
apartment to keep track of developments. On the morning of the
Sudetenland takeover, and in the midst of the excitement created
by reports, later proved false, of fighting between Czech and
German troops, the unlisted copydesk phone rang. It was an
apoplectic Grimes. "Why in the goddamn hell didn't you call
me?" "Too busy and still am," I replied, and hung up.

An hour later Grimes appeared and strolled over to the news
desk, a roll of ticker copy in his hands.

"Nice job," he said, and walked away.

For Grimes this was an abject apology.

Earlier that hectic year, Nazi adventurism produced one of *The Wall Street Journal*'s historic news stories. Although we had a reliable part-time correspondent in Berlin, Charles Hargrove, our Paris Bureau chief, decided that the situation demanded his personal presence.

On March 12, 1938, the day after Hargrove arrived, Hitler's army marched into Austria. Tight outgoing censorship was clamped down. However, Hargrove, a British national, talked a friend in the embassy into including a brief and hurried dispatch in an outgoing diplomatic pouch. In this fashion, Hargrove's story reached Paris; was delivered by special messenger to our office; thence was urgently cabled to New York.

I rewrote the brief cable, fleshed it out with background and "interpretation" and scheduled it for a lead position on page one of the *Journal*. Grimes demurred. He wanted it condensed and carried as the lead item in the "What's News" summary. "Not the *Journal*'s type of story."

Just then, Casey Hogate arrived for his regular daily visit to the newsroom. He picked up a copy of my story from Grimes' desk and absorbedly read it to the end. "This is just the sort of thing we need more of," he declared enthusiastically.

"You two are ganging up on me," said Grimes.

"Oh," said the unsuspecting publisher, "what were you going to do with it?"

"Page one, column one," replied Grimes with a grin.

This was a real breakthrough, a primitive prototype of the "leader"-type article which was to become the hallmark of *The Wall Street Journal*. It was the first time an offbeat story, by *Journal* standards, had been given top display.

The next morning brought a phone call from Kilgore. "How did you wangle that one past Brother Grimes?"

I explained I had had the powerful, albeit innocent, support of Hogate.

No one who was a Dow Jones' newsman in the late 30s will ever forget the most dramatic and violently shocking news beat ever to rock the financial community. I was strolling toward the ticker news desk one March morning of 1938 when the managing editor, Edward Costenbader, normally the calmest of men under pressure began wildly beckoning to me. Perspiration was running down his chalk-white face. I arrived on the dead run.

With hand over the phone mouthpiece he whispered, "Get hold of Richard Whitney's office [Whitney was a former president of the New York Stock Exchange], and see if he is talking to Dow Jones. I've got a guy on the phone who claims to be Whitney."

This was standard technique. The first rule on any of our news desks was, never take a phone call at face value. I got Whitney's office; identified myself; asked to talk to Mr. Whitney. "Why," his secretary replied, "he's talking to Mr. Costenbader at Dow Jones right now. I placed the call myself."

I turned to Eddie. "It's Whitney on your phone."

Eddie said, "Thanks, Mr. Whitney," hung up, and bellowed at the teletype operator sitting beside him. "Break! Break! Richard Whitney confesses to fraud."

The operator cut into the middle of a transmission and flashed Ed's headline.

That's how the world learned that the former president of the New York Stock Exchange, a member of a distinguished Wall Street dynasty, was en route to the district attorney's office to turn himself in for misappropriating securities belonging to customers. Whitney had called Dow Jones to confess. What motivated him, I do not know. Perhaps he just wanted to do a final favor for a news organization he knew and liked.

Grimes not only achieved a reformation in the *Journal*'s news content, but at the suggestion of our veteran editorial page editor, Thomas F. Woodlock, sponsored an entirely new headline style.

Since the mind of man ran not to the contrary, top news stories in the *Journal* had appeared under a one-column, two-line, all capitals headline. The most talented headline writer was hard pressed to give more than a vague general impression of the story's subject matter. The maximum count per line, each letter and space being one unit, was 12 units.

I was newly appointed Grimes' assistant managing editor when Woodlock advanced his radical theory that a headline should alert the reader as to the article's content. "Tom's right," said Grimes to me. "See what you can do."

The result of my labors was the headline style still used by *The Wall Street Journal.* Now orthodox, in its time this "dress" represented a bold break with tradition. Capital and lowercase was substituted for the all capital letters; requirements for balance and full lines were done away with. On page one, bold italic type, underlined, was used to set the theme of an article. Similar headline liberalizations were standardized for inside stories. Headlines of this type can be specific and give the reader an accurate summary of an article's content. They have the added merit of being quickly and easily written.

Thus, although the present-day *Wall Street Journal* bears only a general family resemblance in content to the newspaper produced under Grimes, its physical appearance is basically unchanged, except that the advertising has vanished from page one.

Grimes' energetic leadership resulted in a highly superior financial newspaper, more newsy, better written and edited, and far better organized. The financial community greeted the improvements with enthusiasm, but had little else to offer in the way of support. Circulation and advertising showed no improvement. The *Journal* already had what little was available of both. The problem was basic. The industry served by *The Wall Street Journal,* battered by the stock market crash and decimated by the ensuing depression, no longer was sizable enough, or prosperous enough, to support a first-class financial daily. Wall Street was a dirty name to the American public, and few indeed wanted to venture into securities investing or to read news affecting securities. Dow Jones as a company eked out a precarious living from the eroded profits of its News Service, by then its only solvent operation.

Casey Hogate presided over a Spartan regime. In the 30s, he was forced to institute a series of staff-wide salary cuts and even "Scotch weeks," vacations without pay.

When I joined the *Journal* staff in 1933, and indeed into the early 1940s, rigid economy was the watchword. No reporter could make a toll call to a news source without prior specific approval of the managing editor. Cables from our foreign bureaus were limited to 25 words, maximum, unless the subject matter was truly urgent. Copy paper on which reporters typed their stories was fabricated laboriously from odds and ends of newsprint "waste" from the pressroom. The typewriters themselves were cranky Woodstock "seconds," traded by the maker for advertising space. The *Journal* carried a substantial volume of hotel and restaurant advertisements. But few such ads were paid for in cash; most were inserted on a "due bill" basis. That is, receipts were issued which could be used for rooms, food, and drinks. These "due bills" were parceled out to deserving staff members in lieu of pay increases. They financed many a vacation trip, including the honeymoon of Bob Feemster, then a rising young star in the advertising sales department, and now and again they provided very welcome free dinners for members of the staff required to work at night.

I recall that Casey Hogate once messaged Washington advising that a large due bill on the Willard Hotel was about to expire. "Everyone eat and drink at Willard; have fun. Regards KCH."

For a week the Washington staff stuffed themselves in the hotel's gourmet dining room, lunch and dinner. And at dinner, always the best French wines.

Dow Jones' annual report for 1940, a couple of mimeographed pages (the Bancroft family then owned some 98 percent of the company's stock), provides some significant benchmarks.

The *Wall Street Journal* (the New York edition) in that year had a daily circulation of 28,000, actually a few thousand less than its companion weekly publication, Barron's. The Pacific Coast Edition, then treated as a separate newspaper, claimed an "estimated" 3,000 more.

Gross revenues of the company were roundly $2 million, and net income for the year, $69,000.

Stubbornly, and in defiance of all financial logic, the *Journal* continued to publish an edition in San Francisco for the few hundred subscribers who actually paid their bills. There were two other financial dailies in the Dow Jones group, both deep in red ink and both surviving on a diet of family sentiment and News Service-derived subsidies. These were the *Boston News Bureau*, which competed for New England readers with the Journal, and the *Philadelphia Financial Journal*, a four-page sheet.

On the plus side, there was not one penny of debt.

And, greatest asset of all, Dow Jones and *The Wall Street Journal* had emerged from the scandals and wheeler-dealing of the stock market boom era with an unblemished reputation for ethical and honest handling of the news.

Despite its shrunken readership and bedraggled finances, *The Wall Street Journal* still enjoyed enormous prestige in both business and governmental circles. This high regard extended to its staff. When I shifted over from the United Press, I quickly discovered that covering Washington, and particularly the government's financial agencies, was a lot easier for a representative of the *Journal*. I had entrée anywhere. Also, I automatically became an "expert," one who could be trusted to competently handle the most technical of news developments. From time to time, I would get a phone call from the Treasury asking if I would "find it convenient" to review the wording of some announcement or other dealing with monetary or banking affairs.

At President Roosevelt's press conference on the first budget message of his administration, he was asked some technical questions. "Read *The Wall Street Journal*" he replied. "Everything you want to know is in there."

Everyone knows the old newspaper joke about the Boston butler who announced "A gentleman from the *Transcript* and some newspaper fellows." Something very similar happened to me in my early Washington days with the *Journal*. Newsmen covering the Treasury asked for a meeting with Secretary William Woodin, Henry Morgenthau's predecessor. The receptionist ushered us into the secretary's private office and announced: "Mr. Kerby of *The Wall Street Journal* and some reporters."

Staff morale, despite low pay and long hours, also was remarkably high. Both Hogate and Grimes were the sort of magnetic leaders who engendered deep loyalty, and "The Family" (the Bancrofts) in Boston were not regarded as remote, absentee owners but with very real, personal affection. All of us shared the same leaky lifeboat. The times, we were well aware, were as lean for owners as for employees.

In the winter of 1937, the news staff demonstrated its loyalty to management and ownership in a concrete way. The New York Newspaper Guild, in those days regarded as far leftist, made a determined effort to organize the news staff of the *Journal,* using promises that a union could improve both pay and working standards.

A spontaneous opposition organized. Buren McCormack, then a reporter specializing in banking news, spearheaded the movement and personally recruited me as a charter member of the independent union which he was forming to contest a Labor Board election with the Guild. When the ballots were counted after some months of mass meetings and intensive electioneering, the Dow Jones Employees Association won by an overwhelming majority and was recognized, albeit somewhat grudgingly, by the Labor Board as bargaining agent. Since renamed the Independent Association of Publisher's Employees, this independent union has continued to represent most Dow Jones white-collar employees.

11

The Kilgore Revolution

THIS was the company, the newspaper, and the staff when Bernard Kilgore took over as managing editor of the *Journal* in February 1941. The minuses were highly tangible, and could be summed up in a few words: "No money and a decimated audience." The assets were highly intangible. If ever a man faced a bootstrap operation, it was Barney Kilgore.

For many months, Barney had been deluging Casey Hogate and Grimes with memos urging radical changes in *The Wall Street Journal*'s news content and editorial format. He used examples from the Washington Bureau's news file to illustrate his ideas in specific fashion. A prime example was the pioneering column, "Washington Wire."

This sprightly weekly column of "inside" news and comment was the first such feature to find a place in the *Journal*. When Kilgore became managing editor, similar weekly special columns were invented for every publishing day.

The arrival of the first "Washington Wire" was the signal for yet another amiable, but heated, argument with Henry Grimes. He felt that its place was the editorial page. Kilgore and I argued for page one. Grimes finally agreed, but on the basis that only the initial column would run in that position to "advertise" the new feature. Then back to the editorial page.

"Washington Wire" was an immediate success. We had dozens of phone calls from readers, a deluge for those days.

The next week I suffered a convenient loss of memory and again ran the new feature on page one. Kilgore, of course, was delighted. Grimes registered a pro forma protest. "You and

Barney are ganging up on me. But I'll agree, the readers like it."
Once again the publisher, Casey Hogate, had been supportive,
without knowing he was siding against his managing editor.

A few months before Kilgore's scheduled arrival in New York,
Grimes told me the news. He added that he would become editor
and devote much of his time to building up the editorial page of
the *Journal.* For me, Grimes said, this meant that I would lose my
job as assistant managing editor. He felt Barney should be free to
pick his own team. Grimes planned to transfer me to Washington
eventually. However, for the next few months I would be on
special reportorial assignment and pretty much free to develop
my own story ideas.

I told Grimes I was delighted with Kilgore's selection;
welcomed the roving reporter assignment; and would be happy,
when the time came, to transfer to Washington.

Good news stories for the *Journal* were everywhere. The
nation was fast moving into a defense-oriented economy. The
draft was creating manpower shortages, and scarcities in basic
materials were already becoming critical.

A series of trips into heavily industrialized areas along the
Eastern seaboard produced material for a number of page one
articles. To pacify Grimes, I contrived some sort of spot-news
lead for each, but I also tried to thoroughly background them and
forecast future trends. Grimes thought they were fine, and my
new boss-to-be dispatched applauding notes from Washington.
Typical of these articles were one forecasting allocations of cop-
per supplies, another predicting an impending shortage in
aluminum, a third dealing with the fantastic expansion of the
machine tool industry, and a fourth featuring the problems of
harassed businessmen in quest of materials allocations.

Barney appeared in New York. Following up on Grimes'
orders, my wife and I started packing for the transfer to Washington. His second day on the job, Kilgore asked: "What's this I
hear about you going to Washington?" I replied that Fanny was
happy packing for a return to her home base.

"Tell Fanny to unpack," said Kilgore. "I need you here. I have
Gene Duffield in Washington."

A few days later, on February 14, Hogate issued his historic notice to the staff. In it he confirmed the ill-kept secret that "in a few days some changes will be effective in the newsroom."

The announcement went on to name Grimes as editor and Bernard Kilgore as managing editor. Eugene Duffield would succeed Kilgore as head of the Washington Bureau, and William F. Kerby "will take charge of some new features which are being developed for the first page of *The Wall Street Journal.*"

Casey's memo added a reassuring note: "While this seems a sizable change, all the personalities are well and favorably known to the entire staff, and everyone affected . . . is in hearty approval."

He concluded by asking for the staff's "usual hearty cooperation."

Thus was the impending "Kilgore revolution" officially disclosed to a suspicious and nervous news staff. Certainly many, probably the majority, did not accord the new regime "hearty approval," and "hearty cooperation" was won grudgingly and only after many, many months of painstaking educational labors.

In explaining my new job to me, Kilgore said he also wanted me "to keep my hand in on the management side." "Do your reporting and writing during the week, and on Sundays you will be in charge of getting out the paper." He explained he didn't want to start his new career as managing editor by immediately countermanding Grimes on the assistant managing editor job.

So I continued to do some special assignment work, including a collaboration with Gene Duffield on a series of articles on the "Defense Economy." The series was in mid-career at the time of Pearl Harbor, when the title was promptly changed to the "War Economy." They were the last articles under my by-line published by the *Journal.* (My father reminded me that he had written a similarly titled series for Scripps after the United States entered World War I.)

One of the hallowed traditions of the *Journal* which Grimes had not changed, reputedly stemming from the Puritan Sabbath ethic, was the practice of setting type for the Monday issue on Saturday. A skeleton staff of four printers worked on Sunday, making corrections and setting the "What's News" page one summary. Barney Kilgore decided this was a practice which, sooner or later, would cause a problem. Thus it was that on December 7, 1941, the *Journal* had a fully manned composing room and copydesk for the first Sunday in its long history.

I was, as usual, in charge of Sunday operations. But Barney also came in to see how the new system would work. A bit after 3:00 P.M., bells began clanging on the entire battery of press association teletype machines. The Japanese had attacked Pearl Harbor.

The news staff reported en masse, some summoned but many arriving before they could be located and called. The historic front page of *The Wall Street Journal* that they produced was a staff effort which I am convinced signaled to the worlds of business and journalism that the "new" *Wall Street Journal* had achieved a certain maturity.

I had just cleared the last of the page one articles for the first edition when Barney turned to me and said: "Now write the lead piece." It was 30 minutes before deadline.

My effort was typed in paragraph "takes" and, with Casey Hogate reading over his shoulder, copyread by Kilgore. Factually, it drew heavily on my reportorial work in progress on the "Defense Economy" series. I was, and still am, proud of the accuracy of its economic and industrial forecasts—rationing, the massive channeling of industrial capacity into war-related products, manpower scarcities, and all the rest.

Pearl Harbor Day was the last time I was to see Casey Hogate in his beloved natural habitat, the newsroom. Suffering from extremely high blood pressure, Casey was impatiently enduring a crash diet of boiled rice and papaya juice and, acme of indignities, no bourbon! Soon after, he had one of a series of strokes, and gradually he withdrew from the company's operations, although he remained its titular head as chairman until his death at Palm Springs, California, on February 11, 1947.

A tireless worker, Hogate put in a standard 16-hour day at his Dow Jones desk, but he also found time to be a moving spirit of the committee which planned the reorganization of the New York Stock Exchange. (He declined a proffered appointment to be its first full-time paid president, a position which went to the much younger William McChesney Martin, who later became chairman of the Federal Reserve Board and a highly valued director of Dow Jones.)

Hogate also served as the unpaid mayor of Scarsdale, New York. On Sundays he batted in the cleanup spot on a Westchester softball team, known as the "Nine Old Men," perennial opponents of a team of New Deal bureaucrats organized by Casey's friend and neighbor, President Franklin D. Roosevelt.

Once the 300-plus-pound Casey lined a titanic hit over the head of the leftfielder, but only managed to lumber to first base.

Twitted by the president on his lack of speed, Hogate replied:

"That's the way it is with us businessmen under the New Deal. We have to hit a home run to get to first base."

Roosevelt roared with laughter and promptly replaced his pitcher, the redoubtable Harry Hopkins.

A few months before Pearl Harbor I had officially assumed, for the second time, the mantle of assistant managing editor. Also, when Kilgore charged me with the task of producing, or supervising the production of, all news articles and feature columns for page one, he gave me the choice of anyone on the New York staff to act as my assistant. I opted for Buren McCormack, an astute newsman and facile writer, who then was heading up banking coverage. As I followed Kilgore up the corporate ladder in the years to come, Mac followed me, serving as my assistant managing editor, managing editor, and executive editor, and he was executive vice president and a director of the company at the time of his death.

The *Journal's* new front page was to be the keystone in Kilgore's program to remake *The Wall Street Journal.* Barney called it "our showcase."

He had come to his position as managing editor with well-defined ideas of what he wanted to achieve, but the methodology and techniques were, of necessity, on a trial and error basis.

Basically, he envisioned a newspaper which would appeal to a much broader audience, the whole business community. He also advocated a nontechnical writing style. "Don't write banking stories for bankers. Write for the banks' customers. There are a hell of a lot more depositors than there are bankers."

Barney wanted a national newspaper. "The businessman in Portland, Oregon, and the businessman in Portland, Maine, need the same information." From this developed his slogan: "For *The Wall Street Journal,* all news is national. If it's important enough to run in any edition, it's important enough to run everywhere."

Also: "It doesn't have to have happened today to be news."

He decreed the elimination of "today" and "yesterday" from leads on *Wall Street Journal* stories. "If a date is essential, use the exact date."

He waged unrelenting warfare on clichés, as witness his famed bulletin board notice, posted after he became president and publisher and had moved upstairs to the faded grandeur of the executive penthouse:

"If I read 'upcoming' in *The Wall Street Journal* once more, I'll be 'downcoming' and someone will be 'outgoing'!"

Kilgore was adamant in his insistence that it was not enough just to produce better stories on the same news developments all the other papers were covering. ("Grimes tried that, and it didn't work.") The *Journal's* front page must be useful, but also it must be interesting and, if possible, amusing and, above all, unique.

"The easiest thing in the world for any reader to do is to stop reading."

"Hook 'em with an intriguing, mystery lead, and keep sinking in more hooks as you go."

This resulted in such page one lead paragraphs as:

"Do you like potato juice? You'll learn to love it in the days ahead." A story on an impending wartime ban on the use of grain in making alcoholic beverages.

Also, "John Jamieson has cancelled the standing order for flowers for his office." A story about the impact of high federal withholding taxes.

And: "The AFL-CIO will see you on the funny pages." A story about a large-scale union labor public relations campaign.

Barney's theories on news treatment and my up to then lonely efforts to produce readable, thoroughly back-grounded articles on timely, although not necessarily spot-news, subjects fit hand-in-glove. McCormack, of course, had been an early and enthusiastic convert to the Kilgore program.

Perforce, and for what seemed an interminable period, Mac and I between us wrote, or rewrote, every article and feature column which appeared on page one of the *Journal*. "What's News" was the sole exception. Perry TeWalt had continued to produce that news summary with a sure professional touch until he was dispatched to Ottawa to start a bureau in the Canadian capital. His successor, another of the omnipresent DePauw alumni, was Maynard Lemon, who proved equally skillful.

Thus it was that I became the first of a line of page one editors. In those early days, standards of quality ranged from fairly good to just barely passable, but at least the articles were different enough to attract attention and, early on, brought a flattering offer from a Scripps feature service for "second-day rights."

The money would have been extremely handy. Barney talked it over with me, and we agreed the offer must be rejected because syndication would kill the *Journal* as the national newspaper we hoped it would become. To the best of my knowledge, the harassed folks worrying about meeting the payroll never knew the offer had been made.

In addition to producing six front pages a week (there was a Saturday edition then) and dredging up the story ideas for those articles, Mac and I also conducted writing classes for reporters. It was urgently necessary to win converts on the news staff who had the writing skills to produce stories which didn't have to be reworked from stem to stern. A few *Journal* staffers early, and successfully, embraced the new techniques. Others were willing, but lacked the writing ability. Most were balky and resentful. Eventually, we had a small cadre of reliables. One was Joseph Guilfoyle, still active as executive editor of the Dow Jones News Service, who became a prolific source of good leaders. Another was the late Frank Dezendorf, whose features had a delightful light, rather folksy, touch. Then there was Robert Bottorff, who recently died in retirement after rising to the position of vice president and general manager of Dow Jones.

There was an important fourth, a lanky ex-cowhand from Oklahoma who loved martinis and classical music and had a gift for clean, incisive writing. This was John O'Riley. John had been laboring, for lack of any other job, as secretary to Cy Kissane, the deposed managing editor of the *Journal.*

Among other marginal tasks, Kissane produced a feeble weekly imitation of the Kiplinger Letter. I had the unenviable chore of editing this product and attempting to convert it into something which would convince subscribers they were getting some sort of insight into political and economic affairs. One week I was astounded to receive a well-written, concise, and interesting version. The explanation—Kissane was home nursing a cold, and his secretary had produced it.

I immediately engineered O'Riley's transfer to the news staff. There he had a long and highly productive career despite a serious heart condition which, in later years, precluded the strain of executive duties. At the time of his retirement in 1977, John was a highly respected economic writer for the *Journal* and contributed regularly to the page one "Outlook" column.

My teaching technique for the staff was most unacademic and highly direct. Any reporter with a major story in hand was required to orally summarize it for me before attempting to put it on paper. At first, the odds were astronomical that the version coming from his typewriter would bear little or no resemblance to the story as he had told it to me.

"Now, Tom," I would say, "this isn't the way you told me the story. The first thing you mentioned was a near riot at that stockholders' meeting. What happened to the riot?"

"Oh," he replied, "the company's earnings forecast is what our readers really want to know about."

I would reply in effect: Go back and write it the way you told it to me. What you thought would most interest me will most interest our readers.

From this type of interview arose the editorial dictum:

"Talk your story; don't write it."

We also emphasized some simple precepts of good writing. Try for a short, punchy lead. Avoid run-on sentences. Intersperse short sentences with long ones. A one-sentence paragraph is no sin. Periods and semicolons are great inventions. And so on. We also fought against what we called "lazy words." *Virtually* was my particular bête noire.

It was my bulletin board notice to the staff which said:

"From today on there will be virtually no virtuallys used in *The Wall Street Journal*."

We also invented a system of standard translations of unavoidable technical terms. These were placed in a card index at the copydesk. Such terms as *arbitrage, the Bombay straddle, prime rate,* and *gray goods* were always followed by a brief parenthetical explanation in lay language.

Another of our early journalistic inventions was the so-called all-cities roundup, the bane of the reportorial staff because by definition it was hard and anonymous work. The *Journal* shared a network of news bureaus with the Dow Jones News Service. This made it possible to do a very rapid nationwide survey story when some news event, or economic trend, indicated its desirability. In essence, our roundups were highly unscientific, but usually quite accurate, Gallup-type efforts.

We set some sort of record, probably for all time, the first day wartime food price controls went into effect. I assigned 50 newsmen, with wives if available, to go shopping for a designated market basket of foodstuffs. Twelve cities were covered in this way. My shoppers reported what they were charged, and checked prices against the official Office of Price Administration ceilings. The story was a blockbuster.

We had won some converts on the news staff but had a long way to go when out of the blue came help. An academic friend wrote me to report that Robert Gunning, a professor at the University of Toledo, was delivering lectures on clear, good writing, using *The Wall Street Journal*'s front page as a prime example. He had invented a grading system, based on comprehension at various reading levels. The *Journal's* page one leaders averaged age-12 comprehension. Incidentally, so, he said, did Dickens' novels, Hemingway's short stories, Eugene O'Neill's plays, and other literary classics.

The professor agreed to come to New York and deliver a series of talks to the news staff. He was persuasive and convincing. With one sentence he destroyed the prevalent doctrine of staff dissidents that the new techniques involved "writing down" to *Journal* readers. "If you are writing down to your readers, then so does Hemingway."

It would be pleasant to report that all this journalistic pioneering resulted in an instant circulation explosion for *The Wall Street Journal*. It did not. Initially the *Journal* created much more excitement in journalism circles than among our desired readers. There were several reasons. The paper inevitably suffered from being regarded as a financial trade paper, catering to brokers and bankers only. Second, timely distribution was difficult except along the Northeastern seaboard and in California. The final and crushing blow to growth was the imposition of newsprint rationing as a wartime measure. This all but eliminated circulation promotion. Thus, when the war ended in 1945, the *Journal's* readership was under 60,000 daily. The 100,000 mark was not reached until 1947.

Advertising was becoming relatively much more plentiful. Companies were gorged with military orders. The imposition of the excess profits tax was a heavy artificial stimulant. Might as well spend the money on advertising, which may do us some good later, rather than give it to the government. Such was the reasoning of many a corporate executive.

The *Journal* strictly limited the amount of advertising it would carry, and we devoted every pound of newsprint we could dredge up to building readership. While the circulation pressure was far from overwhelming, it had become obvious that there were indeed potential new readers who wanted the kind of newspaper the *Journal* was in process of becoming. A professional marketing survey revealed that we were acquiring a sizable secondary readership for each copy available.

When Barney was named general manager of Dow Jones on December 30, 1942, and I succceded him as managing editor, he gave me the added chore of husbanding our meager supplies of newsprint.

The old saw "Necessity is the mother of invention" was never more apt than in the matter of the *Journal's* adoption of a "news formula." Initially this was a technique for economizing on paper. It was only later that it dawned on me that I had given birth to a foolproof method of exercising editorial discipline, improving the quality of the *Journal*, and saving untold sums in production costs.

The idea was simple. I reviewed some 30 issues of the *Journal* and reedited every story of any substantial length. I then proceeded to my mathematical calculations and arrived at the average number of columns per day needed to present tightly edited news in adequate fashion. I issued a ukase to the copydesk. From now on, the *Journal* would contain no more than 54 columns (nine pages) of news content. This included complete market quotations and a half (three-column) editorial page. The *Journal*, then as now, was a six-column paper.

The only individual with the authority to vary from this formula was the managing editor personally. Under very exceptional circumstances, when the flow of news was extremely heavy, I would take extra space. But such occasions were very rare in wartime.

The results were startling. The *Journal* became a much better edited, more concise, meatier newspaper. Filler stories, which our readers didn't really want, or need, were completely eliminated. Our composing rooms knew exactly how much type they had to set each night, and weren't forced to staff for the occasional "big" papers.

Starting with the basic nine pages, the day's quota of advertising was added, and this determined the actual size of each issue. If we thought we could afford the newsprint to run a 16-page issue, that meant 42 columns of advertising and 54 columns of news. All Americans had become accustomed to rationing, so when we explained to advertisers that we needed "options" to run their ads, they cooperated and would give us a list of optional desired dates.

As of this writing, the *Journal* is still operating on a news-formula basis, but obviously one tremendously expanded from that original 54 columns.

The *Journal* was not only short of newsprint (quotas were based on prior consumption) but was rapidly drained of manpower. The only newsmen in a draft-exempt category were "managing editors of general newspapers." Our younger newsmen departed almost en masse. The copydesk in particular was decimated.

Barney dispatched letters to the deans of a dozen journalism schools, asking for the names of their most promising recent women graduates who had actually gone into newspaper work. The deans were cooperative, and I acquired a sizable list of prospects. We didn't even bother with interviews, but offered permanent jobs at good salaries. Almost all of the women on our list were working on very small papers, some on weeklies. Eight liked the idea of moving to metropolitan journalism, and accepted out of hand.

Two newspaper veterans in their 60s were dredged up to give experience to the "beauty chorus," as the staff called the women recruits. I have never worked with a more efficient, dedicated group. By some eight years later, all had departed, most because they preferred marriage to a professional career. But in every instance the resignations were voluntary and regretted. Not one left for another newspaper job.

By the winter of 1942 it had become apparent that Casey Hogate's health had deteriorated to a point where a firm hand was needed at the top of the company. Actually, the change was much overdue.

One night I received a phone call at home from an agitated Henry Grimes. He reported that Hogate was planning to designate a general manager and had proposed the appointment of Joseph Ackell, who was running the production department.

Said Grimes in effect: If they appoint Ackell, I'm going to resign and I think Barney will too. What will you do?

"I'll quit too."

OK, Grimes responded. I'm going to call Jack Richardson in Boston (Richardson was the Bancroft family's attorney and man of business) and tell him just that. Kilgore's the man for the job.

There are, I know, other and less dramatic versions of how Barney Kilgore became the top man in Dow Jones, but this is the way Grimes reported it and the way I'm convinced it was.

Whether Grimes actually used the threat of an exodus of the company's three top news executives, I do not know. He never said.

But I did get a second phone call.

"Come on over."

I found Kilgore with him. All three of us lived in Brooklyn Heights.

Said Grimes: Barney's in as general manager. I stay as editor and keep an eye on all news operations, and you are the new managing editor of *The Wall Street Journal*. Who do you want as assistant managing editor?

I replied, McCormack, of course.

Fine, said Grimes. Your salary goes to $150 a week. (I was making $115.)

What about a raise for Mac?

No money for that, replied Grimes.

Can I take a raise of $20 and give Mac one of $15?

Sure, if you want to.

That was the way Henry Grimes engineered the appointment of one of his subordinates to the top spot in Dow Jones. True or not, I later heard that he had been offered the general manager's job but had rejected in favor of Barney as better qualified. If he did indeed receive such an offer, I am sure he would have refused it, and for just that reason.

It is all but impossible to convey the atmosphere pervading the newsroom as the Kilgore revolution began to take hold of the staff. There was electricity in the air, intense excitement, and a growing conviction that here was the program, and the leadership, which would revitalize a newspaper which many, in and out of Dow Jones, believed had been suffering from a terminal illness.

An elderly journalism professor who visited the newsroom at 44 Broad Street summed it up:

"I haven't known people to act and talk this way since Henry Luce started *Time*."

There were still a few holdouts on the staff, mostly old-time reporters, who bitterly resented the new techniques, particularly the inevitable rewrite of their stories. They found allies and a focal point in the editing staff of the Dow Jones News Service.

For years "the ticker" had been the kingpin of Dow Jones. It made all the money. Suddenly the *Journal* was the focus of attention.

There was intense competition for reportorial time. The ticker editors, and with justification, felt the staff was neglecting fast spot-news coverage to concentrate on the glamorous work of writing signed articles for the newspaper. There was another significant factor. Then, as now, the Dow Jones News Service was sold to newspapers and press services. If a reporter turned up an exclusive story, the last thing he relished was reading it in some other paper before it could appear in the *Journal*.

A case in point was the historic "Product X" story. This was another, and possibly the most significant, in a long line of exclusives unearthed by science writer Sydney B. Self.

Late one afternoon he ambled up to my desk and in a matter-of-fact way said, "I think I could be on to one of the best news stories I have ever had."

What he was "on to" was ironclad confirmation that Du Pont scientists had invented what later came to be known as nylon, then code-named Product X. Among other things, it very quickly preempted the largest and most profitable markets for natural silk. Moreover, in the war which was to engulf the United States, its invention in 1937 made us and our allies independent of what would have become an unavailable, and highly essential, imported commodity.

With Syd sitting beside me and feeding me information and ideas, I wrote the page one article on Product X. Syd was a greatly talented and highly respected reporter in his specialty, but neither nature nor Princeton University had vested him with the ability to translate his information into written English easily comprehensible to the layman.

The ticker editors went into a frenzy the next morning when they read *The Wall Street Journal*'s front page. Here was a story which devastated prices in raw silk futures, then one of the most important and volatile of commodity markets. Also, the story was enormously bullish on Du Pont stock. The ticker editors found it hard to believe I hadn't known anything about Syd's scoop until well after trading had ended for the day. Frankly, I was most happy I hadn't. Like Syd, I had no desire to read his exclusive in the New York afternoon newspapers and in the other morning papers the next day.

However, it was obvious that, in all good conscience, a workable compromise had to be reached. When I became executive editor in 1945, I promulgated a rule that if any reporter had news which would affect trading prior to the close of the markets, it was essential that the News Service get first crack at it. No holding back, no matter how much it hurt. On the other hand, if the markets were closed, even though the ticker was still operating, we kept exclusives for the *Journal*.

However, if a story would not affect market prices, no matter how interesting or important it might be, *The Wall Street Journal* got first-publication rights.

One exclusive of this type was a remarkable example of reportorial ingenuity on the part of a veteran member of our Boston staff, Lester Smith. Ford Motor Company was then still the privately owned property of the Ford family. Its financial figures were a jealously guarded secret. The curiosity of the financial world as well as other automobile makers had been whetted by recurrent rumors that Ford was considering "going public."

Working with the fragmentary figures which Ford had to file annually with the State of Massachusetts, Smith somehow managed to put together a complete income account. To better conceal his sources, we rounded off every statistic, but, as was later demonstrated, not in such a way as to distort the picture.

Thus, when Ford Motor Company issued a statement saying that not one figure in the *Journal* story was accurate, the company was technically correct. We also were correct when we stated that we had complete confidence in our report. What's a few thousand dollars when you are making untold millions?

To everyone's dismay, our prized exclusive appeared in condensed form the same morning in late editions of the *New York Times*.

The evidence that it was outright theft was clear. The *Times* version used the same slightly altered figures which we had employed to conceal our reporter's sources. The origin of the *Times* information also was not hard to track. Our merchandising people had decided that the most effective promotion for *The Wall Street Journal* was the *Journal* itself. They had used a reproduction of the current day's front page as the basis of an advertisement in the *Times*, and someone on that newspaper's news staff had unabashedly filched our exclusive from the ad after it appeared in an early edition. My old friend, Turner Catledge, by then managing editor of the *Times*, apologized in the next day's paper for this "inadvertent" use, a remarkable bit of semanticism.

12

The Journal in Wartime

As *The Wall Street Journal* commented in a page one article written the night of Pearl Harbor:

"War with Japan means industrial revolution in the United States."

Unquestionably this revolution gave our fledgling national economic newspaper enormous impetus and foreshortened by many years the period required to establish the *Journal* as a major newspaper, the recognized authority on news events affecting American business.

Viewing today's American economy, it is difficult to recall what the American economy was before it became the closely integrated production and marketing machine which emerged from the war. The demands of national defense obliterated most traces of economic regionalism. The same interplay of economic and political forces created an insatiable and urgent demand for information. It was impossible to operate an enterprise in any field, and dangerous to conduct personal business, without access to the most timely economic news.

By grace of Barney Kilgore's ambition to produce America's first national newspaper, the "new" *Wall Street Journal* was available to meet this demand. Thus, a market and a product emerged at the same moment.

The war the *Journal* recorded and interpreted in meticulous detail was not the war of battles and heroism. The Japanese invasion of the Philippines and the Battle of Bataan were covered in a few brief paragraphs in the "What's News" summary of general news events. So too with the fall of Singapore, the Battle of Midway, the Allied landing in Normandy, and all the other news from the fighting fronts which made banner headlines in our sister newspapers.

The *Journal's* war was fought on the home front. Ours was the story of shortages, manpower and materials allocations, rationing, price controls. And, for the first time in its long history, *The Wall Street Journal* recognized its readers as not only managers of business and finance but also consumers. So we tried to be as alert to news affecting them and their families as we were to events important to their business operations.

Obviously, the *Journal* of the war years was far from the highly polished newspaper it is today. The staff was relatively small. Editors and reporters alike were struggling to perfect, and adapt to, revolutionary journalistic techniques. It was produced by methods long since obsolete, and distributed, apart from a few large cities on the two coasts, in a halting and uncertain fashion. But it was the best thing available, really the only game in town.

And it did show steady improvement despite crippling shortages of experienced personnel and newsprint.

No longer did I come to the office on a Sunday morning to find a note from Kilgore or McCormack saying: "Here's one leader; scramble for the other."

Washington early on became a sure source of major stories which were printable (by our then not-too-demanding standards) without major rewrite. In time a few of the news offices, notably the Pacific Coast bureaus, Chicago, and Boston, also were contributing an occasional article which, in our terminology, could be "processed" rather than rewritten from stem to stern.

Thus, by the time I took over the managing editorship in January 1943, McCormack and I were no longer writing all the page one stories. In a pinch we could draft a couple of other newsmen who were competent editors and rewriters.

The wartime *Wall Street Journal's* news coverage concentrated on utility. The rapid and necessarily ruthless transformation of America's industrial complex into a machine whose first priority was supplying the sinews of war created an endless array of unfamiliar problems.

The *Journal* predicted and soon thereafter chronicled the disappearance from the marketplace of consumer durable goods—passenger cars, refrigerators, vacuum cleaners, even bicycles.

Rationing was a big continuing story—meat, sugar, coffee, gasoline, fuel oil for home heating, shoes. Cloth for clothing became scarce. The two-pants, vested suit went the way of such expendables as formal clothing. Cigarettes and liquor were in extremely short supply, and well-known brand names all but unobtainable.

The War Production Board and the Office of Price Administration cranked out orders and directives as fast as their mimeograph machines could operate. The *Journal* early adopted a much-appreciated policy of running a daily digest of all federal government orders and regulations. This utilitarian feature alerted our readers well in advance of the more ponderous official information dissemination system.

So-called voluntary censorship was imposed. Byron Price, a highly respected Associated Press news executive, was put in charge. One of his principal aides was my father. Price, an old friend, induced him to give up his new retired status for the duration. I never learned what my father's real job was. He took an oath never to talk about it, and he never did. I did discover, quite by accident, that he had top security clearance and that all his discarded papers went into a red wastebasket, which meant the contents were run through a shredder and then burned.

Censorship initially was pretty rough and ready. A week or so after Pearl Harbor, the *Journal* was sternly rebuked for (1) running a picture of a huge pile of old auto tires (an "invitation to sabotage") and (2) using some background information garnered from *Encyclopaedia Britannica*. Presumably the theory was that no one in Japan or Germany could or would read a standard reference work.

However, Price soon had things running remarkably smoothly. Any story about which I had the slightest doubt could be precleared by the Office of Censorship. Being manned by experienced newsmen who knew the necessity for speed in news handling, the clearance process was prompt and efficient. If a publication had prior clearance, it was exempt from later harassment and second-guessing by the military authorities.

But, it developed, in the earlier days of the war the military apparatus deemed some things so secret they were concealed from the censors. This policy came to an abrupt halt largely as the result of a *Wall Street Journal* story reporting a major chemical breakthrough. This was the development of silicones, the first successful amalgams of organic and inorganic matter. The reporter concerned vowed on questioning that he knew of no possible specialized military use for the new materials. Nevertheless, I wired the article to the Office of Censorship and promptly received permission to print it as submitted.

This the *Journal* did. The next morning I came to work to find my office populated with stern-faced representatives of the FBI and Army and Navy intelligence. I then learned that all concerned regarded the development of silicones as of such military importance it had been decided to keep the whole matter secret even from the Office of Censorship.

I displayed a copy of the story stamped with the censor's clearance. The intelligence apparatus departed, grumbling but defeated. However, the incident triggered a reform in communications between the military and the censorship office. Soon I, in common with other managing editors and top news executives of the press services, began receiving memoranda marked "Secret. For Your Eyes Only." These detailed particularly sensitive areas and developments which newsmen should avoid in the interests of national security.

The system worked. I do not know of any violations. One prime example of the system's effectiveness involved the Japanese campaign to attack the Pacific Coast with balloon bombs. Balloons bearing an explosive charge were released in Japan. Propelled by the predominant west-to-east air currents over the Pacific, many of the balloons descended on the U.S. West Coast. It was hit or miss, but a number of the charges did explode at or near targets of some importance. Not one word appeared in the newspapers. Discouraged, the Japanese abandoned the campaign.

The *Journal's* most sensational wartime news story obviously never reached the censor's desk. It was never even put on paper.

In the spring of 1943, I met a young scientist whose name I have forgotten if I ever knew it. He was a fellow guest at a large New York cocktail party. To make conversation, I asked if he was doing "anything interesting" these wartime days.

Not really, he replied. I'm just a spear carrier at our testing lab. I'm one of a team working on thick lead shields. They don't tell us much of anything, but I gather the idea is protection against heavy explosions. Anyway, it's a top priority job and I'm lucky to have this weekend off.

Shortly after this conversation *The Wall Street Journal* carried a news item reporting that the Canadian government had ordered trading suspended in two mining companies listed on the Montreal Stock Exchange. No reason was given. Always intrigued by the unexplained, I checked one of the standard manuals. They were the only North American producers of ores from which radium was extracted.

Radium—and lead shields being tested on a top priority basis! Leslie Charteris, my favorite producer of escape literature, had written a spy novel on a scientist who had discovered how to split the atom and produce a devastating explosive.

I dropped by science reporter Syd Self's desk. "Syd, I have a hunch we may have started work on a new weapon or high explosive." I relayed my slender evidence. "Nose around."

Two days later he reported to me in detail on the Manhattan Project.

Obviously, Self and I kept our information to ourselves, but right up to the first test of an atom bomb at Los Alamos, Self, and I through him, followed the program step by step. Then Self's sources of information suddenly dried up. "I think we're coming to the climax."

Aside from satisfying the intense curiosity which is an essential ingredient of every newsman worth his salt, did it do us any good?

Yes, because early on I began preparing for news coverage of the transformation of the American economy from war to peace. When the bomb was dropped on Hiroshima, we were off to a running start.

Barney Kilgore was caught up by the draft soon after Pearl
Harbor, passed his preliminary physical, but, as was not too
unusual, was classified 4-F after taking the more comprehensive
examination conducted by the Army's own doctors. X-rays
showed a severe but arrested case of tuberculosis. He had never
known he had had the disease.

Soon after Pearl Harbor, Navy friends who remembered me
from the days when I had covered the department, offered me a
commission in naval intelligence. When it developed I had had
polio as a small child, the offer was immediately withdrawn. I
never could quite understand how a wonky left leg would have
handicapped me as a press relations officer. But the services
were more fussy in the early days of the war. All naval officers
had to be "fit for combat duty."

When the definitive draft regulations were issued, "managing
editors of general daily newspapers" were one of the very few
categories "exempt as war necessary." This was the recommendation from General Hershey's national headquarters, but by
law local draft boards had the final decision. All of this resulted
in my setting an all-American record for Wasserman tests.

My draft board, ignoring the recommended national policy,
would call me. I would pass a preliminary, and highly casual,
physical, including the standard Wasserman. Then national draft
headquarters would "stay induction" and remind my local board
of the "exempt category" directive.

This process went on and on. But one morning I wound up at
the induction center in Manhattan.

Stripped naked, except for my socks, I first was interviewed by
a master sergeant on the subject of literacy. I assured him I could
read and write. He wanted to know my job in civilian life and
then agreed I had passed the literacy test.

I made my way from one medical station to another, passing all
examinations with flying colors. The next to the last stop was the
psychiatrist. He inquired as to my sexual preferences, and I
assured him I had a firm and active interest in females. Then,
"Any sports preferences?"

I replied, "The same as yours, Dr. Donovan. I play golf a lot, if not well."

"I knew I knew you," said the doctor. "You have a house at Buck Hill Falls. So do I."

Then, "Didn't I see you limping badly when you walked in?"

I replied I had had polio as a child, which had left me with a bad left leg.

He picked up his red pencil (the signal for physical rejection) and heavily underscored a line in the form for "skeletal defect." My next, and last, stop, he explained, was the orthopedic examination, manned on that particular day, he added, by a substitute doctor he described as "too damn casual." "I shouldn't do this, but there's no point in your being inducted and then getting thrown out when the Army gets around to giving you a real physical."

Sure enough, the substitute orthopedist glanced over a group of us and remarked, "Fine specimens. You all pass." He then proceeded to initial the forms we carried. When he came to me, the red pencil underline brought him up short.

"What's this?" I explained that one of the earlier examining doctors had noticed I had a bad leg. He grumbled under his breath, but took a thorough look at me, first walking, then on the examining table. Then he initialed the rejection notation.

Along with my fellow inductees, I reclaimed my clothing. Most moved along to a welcoming breakfast. I followed signs saying "Rejectees this way" and arrived finally at a Red Cross booth. There a young lady inquired if, being unable to fight for my country, I wouldn't volunteer blood for those who could. I replied I would gladly do so, but I had had hepatitis.

Said she: "You aren't much good for anything."

I agreed; found a phone booth; and called Fanny and then Barney Kilgore to report I was still a civilian.

"I'm glad the Army finally made up its mind," commented my pregnant wife.

The war years for me, and, I'm sure, for other news executives of the *Journal*, were a blur of 12-hour days and seven-day weeks. And never a vacation. After the next morning's first edition of the *Journal* was on its way to the presses, McCormack and I, along with one or more staff members assigned to rewrite, would get busy on future page one leader articles. Often we would work until well past midnight.

Dinner would be sent in from the neighboring Schrafft's restaurant. The standard order was any kind of meat sandwich; if no meat available, then cheese; if no cheese available, then anything. Night after night we wound up eating either lettuce or watercress sandwiches! This was a particular hardship for Bob Bottorff, who loathed all vegetables but potatoes and couldn't abide salads. Years after the war ended he was still commenting bitterly on "that goddamn watercress you fed me." Bob was in New York for several months for an indoctrination course in the "new" *Journal*. When he returned to his San Francisco post he carried the message to our West Coast staff with apostolic zeal.

Another consumer of watercress on unbuttered toast was Raymond Cromley, who had been the *Journal*'s correspondent in Tokyo when Pearl Harbor was attacked. Ray had been interned, along with his half-Japanese small son. His wife, a surgeon, was not interned.

Eventually arrangements were made, as I recall, through the good offices of the Swiss embassy in Tokyo for a group of civilians to be repatriated. The State Department included the Cromleys on the list. Ray and his little boy arrived, but the Japanese authorities refused to permit his wife to leave the country. Soon after the surrender, Cromley set off for Japan. He found his wife, but only a short while before her death. Life had not been easy for the wife of an American.

Uniquely equipped by training and experience, Ray wrote a series of authoritative and penetrating articles on the strengths and weaknesses of Japan and the Japanese economy. These attracted the attention of the Army, and shortly thereafter Cromley was commissioned as an intelligence officer. He served with distinction in the Pacific theater, his assignments including a stint as a liaison officer with Mao and the Chinese Communist armies.

In its issue of September 4, 1945, the *Journal*, with black mourning bands surrounding the type, recorded the death of one of its most distinguished staff members, Thomas F. Woodlock. Tom spanned the history of Dow Jones from the time of the founding partners on. Born in Ireland, he had received a thorough classical education. He was the only man I ever knew who read Greek plays in the original for the fun of it.

His editorials and, in later years, the essays he published under the generic heading "Thinking Things Over" gave a unique distinction to the *Journal's* editorial page. They were learned without being pedantic, reflecting a first-class intellect at work. His interests were catholic, but everything he wrote was a variation on a basic philosophy. This centered on the dignity and the rights of the individual as opposed to the steady movement toward governmental authoritarianism. It is no exaggeration to state that Woodlock's philosophy established the tone for *The Wall Street Journal's* editorial page position, a position which has been firmly maintained ever since by a line of distinguished editors—Grimes, Vermont Royster, Joseph E. Evans, and Robert Bartley, the *Journal's* current editor.

Woodlock was deeply saddened by the spread of both Marxism and fascism, and by the rapidly increasing role of the state in the lives of citizens even in democratic countries. Not too long before his death, he remarked to me: "Bill, I'm glad I'm not as young as you. You will live to see sad and terrible things, and I shall not."

Early in the afternoon of his death, Tom called me from his apartment. He explained he was not feeling too well and was working at home. Could he dictate a column to my secretary? He did. His final essay was published in the following morning's *Journal* along with his obituary.

13

The Kilgore Revolution Spreads

WHEN Barney Kilgore took over the operating reins of Dow Jones in 1943, he inherited a thoroughly disoriented administrative structure. It had been running without any consistent direction, and on what momentum it possessed, for several years. For all his talents, Casey Hogate had never learned to delegate. Up to his illness he had made the decisions, many times down to the most minute details.

One example: As president and publisher, he read every word of type printed in *The Wall Street Journal*.

Relays of copyboys would bring marked tear sheets from the first edition down to the copydesk. Typographical errors would be corrected; headlines rewritten; editing changes made, even to rewritten leads. All of this would flood the night editor.

Most corrections would have been made long before those of the one-man copydesk in the presidential penthouse. The only solution was to keep a duplicate set of every alteration made by the copydesk. This was tedious and time-consuming, but the only way to avoid utter chaos in the composing room.

I was familiar only with the news operations, but friends in other departments told me Hogate was just as deeply involved in the details of their operations.

Barney Kilgore was the direct opposite. He was a devoted apostle of delegation. "If a man has the responsibility, he must have the authority."

In 1945, when Kilgore was appointed president, he found himself with the authority to establish a responsible and workable management structure. Four general department heads were named. Grimes retained general control of all news operations; Bob Feemster was put in charge of all sales operations. These included advertising, circulation, and sales of the News Service in the United States and Canada. Joseph J. Ackell headed up production and service operations, including circulation service, which Barney split off from the sales function. The elderly comptroller, Clifford Hoskins, was named treasurer, but he was a department head in name only. For an interim period Barney was pretty much his own business manager, and then a youngish new comptroller was appointed. This was Thomas F. Mowle, an accountant who had been handling the Dow Jones outside audit for the Lybrand firm, now Coopers & Lybrand.

With Kilgore's encouragement, Mowle moved the business office (renamed Accounting and General Office) into the 20th century. To him also must go the credit for either recruiting or encouraging an impressive group of bright young men, many of whom moved on to key executive posts in the Dow Jones organization. The AGO supplied, among others, John J. McCarthy, until recently vice president/administration; Frederick Harris, vice president/finance; Frederick Hetzel, treasurer; and Robert Wilson, circulation service director.

Hoskins officially retired on January 1, 1949, and Kilgore to my consternation assigned me the additional duties of treasurer, making it clear that he expected me to really run the business office. At the same time I remained the operating head of news as executive editor of Dow Jones publications and services. This was a position I had held since 1945, when Buren McCormack succeeded me as managing editor.

If there ever was an example of on-the-job training, my early career as treasurer was it. In time I learned the rudiments of accounting more or less by osmosis. Taxes and insurance were not entirely strange territory. My reportorial assignments had given me some working familiarity with both fields.

Obviously, I left the books strictly to Mowle; also billing and collection procedures and systems. I devoted myself to modernizing the company's chaotic, and expensive, insurance coverage, developing a good program of group life insurance for employees, and to introducing a workable, realistic system of departmental budgets. In all of Dow Jones' long history, no one had ever indulged in budgeting. My reform was received with a marked lack of enthusiasm by some of the more freewheeling department heads. But Barney Kilgore backed me up, and rapped the knuckles of the more recalcitrant, notably Bob Feemster, whose talents as a merchandiser were matched only by his ineptitude at anything verging on mathematics. Personally, he forfeited thousands of dollars a year because he couldn't, or wouldn't, keep any record of his business expenses.

In due course, I also set up the company's first personnel office and drafted John McCarthy from Mowle's department as Dow Jones' first personnel manager. John and I fought the battle of wage and salary controls. I discovered to my delight that in addition to having accounting background, John was an attorney and a member of the New York bar.

By natural evolution, the two of us also became deeply involved in labor union contract negotiations, eventually taking over this function from Joe Ackell. For some years, however, we teamed up with Joe, a skilled and experienced hand at the bargaining table.

It was Joe who taught me that there always must be a "good guy" and a "bad guy" in union negotiations. The bad guy—that was Joe—must be tough, combative, unyielding on even the smallest and most innocuous points. The good guy—that was my usual role—was the compromiser, the one who came up, apparently on the spur of the moment, with some concessions, perhaps even the solution of a major point of dispute.

Another one of Joe's axioms was that negotiators for the company must never appear to have the final authority to say yes or no. Union bargainers, he would point out, don't have that authority. They must get a ratification vote from their members. Therefore, we must not have that authority. His favorite ploy was: We'll recommend it, but you must realize the "directors" must approve. To my positive knowledge, Dow Jones directors have yet to see their first labor contract.

Joe had another maxim, to me the most vital. "Give them money," Joe would say, "but never, never give up the right of management to run the shop. That's the easy way, and the road to disaster." It was this policy which in the early 1950s resulted in my advising the New York Publishers Association that *The Wall Street Journal* was resigning and going on its own in labor negotiations.

Despite wartime restrictions, Barney Kilgore worked tenaciously to move *The Wall Street Journal* toward his goal of a national newspaper. The struggling Pacific Coast Edition was converted into a reasonable facsimile of the parent printed in New York. Inadequate communications and production facilities limited what could be accomplished, but at least several key pages were identical, including the "showcase," page one.

It was not until 1952 that a Joe Ackell invention resulted in the technology which made feasible the publication of multiple *Journal* editions containing identical news and statistical content. By that time the newspaper was being produced in four locations: New York, Chicago, Dallas, and San Francisco.

Intrigued by the possibility of automatic typesetting, Joe set out to develop a remote control electronic method. The "Teletypesetter" was already on the market, but Joe disparaged it as "a clumsy substitution of solenoids for printers' fingers." Besides, "it doesn't set type fast enough to be worthwhile."

One morning in the early spring of 1951, Joe escorted me to his laboratory and machine shop on lower Sixth Avenue. Here was installed a working prototype model of what Joe, a lover of mysteries, had code-named "Mary Ann." A maze of electronic tubes and other gadgetry was mounted on a series of long tables. From them ran an electrical connection to another Rube Goldberg-ish contraption, which in turn was connected with a standard linecasting machine.

The whole apparatus occupied a room some 20 feet square. But it worked. Perforated tape was fed into the first maze, and the linecaster, without aid of human hands, was producing errorless lines of type as fast as Mr. Mergenthaler's invention could be induced to operate.

The next step, Joe explained, was to condense all his apparatus into a commercial model. After that, the standard linecasters would have to be modified so they could be operated at faster than top manual speed.

All of this wound up in Joe's treasured patents with the official designation "Electro-Typesetter."

"I have the machine," said Joe. "Now, what do we do with it?"

Sitting in his laboratory office, the two of us laid out our campaign. The first step, we decided, was to set stock market quotations automatically.

By any manual methods, these pages of statistics were by far the most expensive and the most tedious section of the *Journal* to produce. Quotations generated by the Associated Press arrived on narrow gummed tape, which was sorted and pasted on sheets by a sizable corps of quotations clerks. Then the quotations were set manually and proofread twice, once by printers and once by senior quotations compilers. Despite this care, mistakes were not uncommon, resulting from the human errors inherent in manual type composition.

All well and good. But the Associated Press had to be talked into producing full quotations for automated typesetting. Then the Typographical Union had to let its members work with the new machines.

My old friend Harry Montgomery, assistant general manager of the AP, proved most cooperative. As Dow Jones would be the only customer, he stipulated, and not unreasonably, that initially we pay the whole cost.

The New York local printers union was adamantly opposed. It wouldn't even negotiate the question. But somehow Ackell wangled the dispute into the realm of the International (headquarters) officers. A bargaining team of top officials, headed by the then president of the ITU, Woodruff Randolph, arrived in New York. Another member of the bargaining team, the union's expert on automation, was an ITU vice president by the name of Clark. It developed that he and I had known each other when he played football for Ohio State, a fortunate coincidence.

"Bad man" Ackell led off the discussions. The *Journal* had already placed the new equipment in its New York composing room. "We will use it," said Ackell, "with or without the Typographical Union. We much prefer to work with union journeymen, and we very much hope the union will want to work with these machines. But union or no union, the machines will be operated. The future of Dow Jones depends on it."

As the discussion went on, I concentrated on Clark, my college-days acquaintance. I stressed our ambition to become America's first national newspaper, with identical content, printed in regional plants and distributed in timely fashion to readers all over the United States. I discussed futures. Already we had four publishing centers in operation; in time I could see the possibility of six, perhaps even eight. (I underestimated violently. As of this writing, there are 12 *Journal* plants, and soon there will be 17.) Thus, my argument ran, although an automated *Journal* plant would in time employ fewer than the normal number of ITU members in any one conventional plant, in aggregate we would offer employment to many more than if we were not permitted to automate and grow.

Clark, and eventually the others, bought this line of reasoning. But they were adamant in protecting the jobs of their local union members. They wanted us to guarantee that the number of "situations," regular jobs, in all our composing rooms would never be less than the current number.

"Bad man" Joe hung tough. "Good guy" Kerby, as Joe and I had previously agreed, offered the compromise. No current employees would ever be displaced as a result of automation, but when they left for other reasons, we had no obligation to replace them. Also, for an "experimental" period we agreed to one "machine tender" for each automated machine, in other words a sizable measure of featherbedding. And for the same "experimental" period, only market quotations could be produced by the new equipment.

Not an ideal contract measured against those now generally in force. But we broke the ice, and *The Wall Street Journal* became the first metropolitan newspaper to use automated typesetting.

A year later Ackell negotiated an expansion of the original agreement so that all type used in the *Journal* could be set automatically.

Kilgore had the technology to produce his true national newspaper.

———

As wartime restrictions were lifted, the economy boomed, fueled by an enormous pent-up consumer demand. *The Wall Street Journal* boomed along with the national economy. Circulation, which stood at a newsprint-rationed 59,907 in 1945, had climbed to 153,208 by year-end 1950. The highly successful promotion theme: "Men who get ahead in business read *The*

Wall Street Journal." Bob Feemster and his advertising sales staff had been persistently and successfully hammering home the message that the *Journal* was a national business daily and not a Wall Street sheet of interest only to brokers or bankers. They found managers of businesses much easier to convince than their advertising agencies (by then many of the businessmen were devoted readers). So the technique was to sell the advertiser directly and have the advertiser order its ad agency to place business in the *Journal.*

Independent research produced convincing evidence of the high demographics of the *Journal's* audience. Advertising rates climbed with the circulation.

Anxious not to outgrow his customers, Feemster came up with the concept of regional rates. In other words, an advertiser could use any one *Journal* edition or any combination of editions at appropriate rates. This technique, unique at the time, has since been much imitated by national publications. Thus, the *Journal* avoided the problem which *Time* magazine had faced earlier when its circulation, and perforce its advertising rates, grew so rapidly that many of its original customers were priced out of the market before other, and larger, advertisers could be sold.

When wartime restrictions ended and communications circuits and equipment at long last became freely available, Feemster seized the opportunity to place the Dow Jones News Service on a much firmer financial footing. Joe Ackell, and another of his inventions, also played a major role.

The founding partners, Dow and Jones, bought rights to one of the first practical printing telegraph machines around the turn of the century. Since that time, the company had used machines exclusively of its own manufacture. The circuitry needed to operate them was not compatible with that required by the teletypes manufactured by AT&T. The Dow Jones equipment also was relatively short-range. News had to be relayed from city to city, then retransmitted by operators in each city to nearby customers.

If, in some fashion, Dow Jones and Bell System telegraph printers could be made to operate from the same transmission, these problems would be solved. An operator typing news stories on a keyboard in New York could serve News Service clients all over the continental United States. No longer would brokers in

New York get the news faster than their opposite numbers in Chicago, or Boston, or San Francisco.

Somehow, Joe Ackell again achieved the impossible. One of his proudest exhibits was a letter from a Bell official advising him that AT&T engineers were convinced the problem was insoluble.

So a national news ticker network was achieved. At this point, Feemster moved to the attack. Because we had been unable to offer service to many brokerage offices, we, perforce, had to permit unpaid redistribution of our news. Bob ended all that, to the outraged cries of the financial community.

One morning he had a climactic meeting with a committee representing the brokerage fraternity.

He came back in triumph. "I just told them," said Bob to me, "that the way things had been going we could wind up with one machine in one office and everybody else in the United States getting their news free from that single service.

"Then I told them, maybe that's a good idea for all of us. We'll deliver the news to the Stock Exchange and the Exchange can relay all over. The price, subject to later increases, will be 2 million a year."

A formula was worked out with the brokerage representatives based on curtailing free redistribution and "opportunity for use"; that is, the larger the brokerage firm (the more offices it had), the higher the fee it paid. This policy has stood up over the years against repeated attacks. The Federal Trade Commission has twice upheld it against antitrust allegations.

14

Up, Up and Away

IN January 1947, Laurence M. Lombard, a highly influential Dow Jones director, first broached the idea that it was time for *The Wall Street Journal* to add a third regional publishing plant to the existing New York and San Francisco operations. He suggested "somewhere" in the Southwest. This was a booming area, but one getting second- and even third-day mail delivery of the *Journal.*

Marketing surveys produced glowing forecasts. Dallas, Texas, was selected as the best distribution center, and contracts for a building and equipment were placed.

Barney Kilgore decided that a high-level promotion and get-acquainted tour through the circulation territory of the edition-to-be would help get us off to a flying start. At that time he nursed a deep antipathy to air travel. "If airplanes will leave me alone, I'll leave them alone." So in the fall of 1947 we set off for St. Louis aboard an overnight New York Central train.

Earlier on I had written my friend Ritchie Cring, then heading the public relations department of the Missouri Kansas Texas (Katy) Railroad, advising that we were starting our barnstorming trip from St. Louis and hoped to see him during our stopover.

Ritchie and two porters met us at the door of our Pullman car. After introducing Barney, I said, "Where are we headed? Our train doesn't leave until evening." "That's what you think," said Ritchie. "Follow me."

We followed, and arrived at a private car, attached to the rear of a Katy express freight train. "I'm sorry but you two will have to pay your way. That's the ICC rule. But I think you will be more comfortable this way. Mind if I go along to see the fun?"

We didn't, and we luxuriated in our mobile home away from home. It developed it was Katy chairman Morpha's own private car, and was staffed with a porter and a talented chef. We pulled into Dallas in style, ahead of our schedule.

Barney and I embarked on a round of lunches, cocktail parties, and dinner speeches, first in Dallas, then Fort Worth, and, eventually, west Texas. The last stop was San Antonio.

Everywhere we were received with boundless enthusiasm and hospitality. It seemed the entire state of Texas could hardly wait to embrace a regional printing of *The Wall Street Journal*. Promises of support and cooperation were on the same lavish scale.

One of our Houston hosts took us to lunch at a plush golf club. While we were at the table, an elderly man walked in, clad in stained, baggy slacks and, despite the heat, a brown sweater with gaping holes.

"Who,"said Barney, "is that? He seems out of place."

"That,"replied our host, "is old man Hunt, right now probably the second richest man in the world. The story is that he was wearing that sweater the first time he ever broke 90 and he's been wearing it ever since."

That night we were escorted to a gambling casino located on the outskirts of Houston. But this was a casino with a difference. Our host explained it was a "cooperative club." That is, it was owned by its members, well-heeled Texans who liked to play for high stakes but wanted a fair shake for their money. Thus it was that the slot machines (all dollar) were set for the highest possible payoff; the blackjack rules were liberalized in favor of the players; the roulette wheel was meticulously balanced, and the odds somewhat better than those prevalent in professional establishments.

Still there was some profit after all expenses, we were told. So menu prices in the restaurant, presided over by a cordon bleu chef, had been reduced to nominal amounts. I vividly recall that a Chateaubriand for two was $1.50. Drinks were 25 cents.

Barney and I had been joined in Houston by two of our associates, Bob Feemster and Pete Wert, our production manager in San Francisco, imported to help get the Southwest Edition started. Pete hit the jackpot on his first try, and wound up $250 richer for his evening out.

The next day we set off for San Antonio, again hitched to a Katy freight. This was the high point of the trip for Barney, a devoted railroad buff. The engineer invited him to ride in the locomotive cab and let him blow the whistle for crossings. I took my turn, and it scared the hell out of me. As third man in the cab, I had nothing much to hold onto, and the engineer was really making time, the cab swaying and lurching violently.

En route to San Antonio, Barney inquired if I was feeling as worn-out as he was. I said I sure was. A seemingly endless round of wining, dining, entertaining, and speech-making is the most exhausting of chores.

"I think we deserve a vacation." We debated the merits of New Orleans, Galveston, etc. Then Ritchie Cring stepped in with a suggestion. It developed he was on friendly terms with a widow who owned the Gallagher ranch, outside San Antonio, a huge spread (one of the original Spanish land grants) and definitely a working cattle operation. Barney embraced the suggestion with enthusiasm, as did Bob Feemster, who had joined up for the last leg of the tour. I had my doubts. To paraphrase Barney, my feeling was, if horses would leave me alone, I'd sure leave them alone.

However, we wound up at the Gallagher ranch the next evening. We were roused at 5:00 A.M., fed an enormous breakfast in company with the cowhands. This featured fruit, orange juice, oatmeal with heavy cream, pancakes, bacon, fried eggs, sausage, and biscuits. All washed down with black coffee served in pint-sized mugs. At six we were in the saddle. Barney Kilgore was an experienced horseman; Feemster had ridden; I had never been closer to a horse than the mount of the Fort Myer trooper who had pursued me during the bonus riots in 1932.

My steed was an apparently amiable and aged cow pony. But he had some personality traits which I found discouraging. Despite my urging, he would amble up the slightest grade but race downhill at breakneck speed. Also, and this verged on the traumatic, when he saw a stray steer he would take off after him at top speed without any volition on my part, After all, he was well aware we were on roundup. Miraculously, we never parted company.

I was on my mount from 6:00 A.M. until 3:00 P.M., with a half-hour break at noon. My triumph came that evening. Barney and Bob Feemster were nursing aching muscles. I, who had never ridden before in my life, hadn't a single ache or pain. I approached the second day in the saddle with moderate enthusiasm, they with reluctance. My one disappointment was that pictures taken of my riding in triumph never reached me. My wife Fanny has always regarded my account of this segment of my Texas adventures with extreme skepticism. I referred her to Kilgore. "I can't trust either one of you in such matters. You always back each other."

It was decided to establish Dallas news and sales offices well in advance of planned publication. I began casting around for a news manager. But none of the senior men on the *Journal* had the slightest interest in moving to Texas. John O'Riley, a native Oklahoman, was a prime candidate. Said John: "I worked like hell to get out of that damned country, and I won't go back voluntarily." A series of equally emphatic refusals turned my search to the reporting staff.

I settled on Larry Farrell, an able young reporter with good news contacts in the oil industry. He was energetic, well organized, and, when I broached the assignment to him, highly enthusiastic. I rounded up a staff for him, largely drawing on the New York and Chicago news bureaus. What I didn't realize when I picked Farrell was that I was also picking a man who would, of sheer necessity, also have to function as production manager, business manager, circulation director, and, for a time, advertising production manager.

In retrospect, it is difficult to imagine a mistake which could have been made by the New York hierarchy that wasn't made in setting up the pioneering Dallas operation.

Joe Ackell decided to subcontract the production operation, engaging the commercial printing firm of Jaggers, Childs & Stovall. Although we had our own building, all printers, stereotypers, and pressmen were employees of the printing company. There was no Dow Jones production manager, and Jaggers never appointed a mechanical superintendent with overall authority.

Some six weeks before scheduled start-up, the advertising sales manager had one lonely signed space contract. But he reported, "Don't worry, I have never met with such enthusiasm." Bob Feemster decided we couldn't meet the payroll with Texas enthusiasm and the ad manager departed, to be replaced by Albert Anastasia, a young, energetic, and highly competent salesman who had started his career as a *Journal* reporter.

A month before start-up, I went to Dallas. I found our building was weeks behind schedule. Except for the press, equipment deliveries were badly, almost fatally, delayed. Perforce, we moved in a week before the announced date of our first edition. We had no office furniture; only temporary flooring in the office areas; no ceilings; no partitions; no air conditioning (Dallas can be mighty hot in May). There was one working telephone, a good 75 yards from the office area. Worst of all, the plumbing hadn't been completed.

I arranged for the use of the toilet facilities in a hospitable factory a block and a half away, and told the building contractor to concentrate all his efforts on the production area. The first priority was a place to install the machinery. In due time, the press, a small tubular with a top speed of 8,000 newspapers an hour, was set up, and so was the sterotyping equipment. But the typesetting machines were on a Katy freight car stranded somewhere between St. Louis and Dallas. God only knew where; the railroad certainly didn't.

They finally appeared, 72 hours before our first edition was scheduled to go to press. We never did manage more than a chaotic, partial dry run, and I discovered to my horror that only one of our printers had ever set stock market tabular matter before, a highly specialized skill. The metal pots on the linecasters were gas-fired. I called the local utility to have the gas turned on. "No can do, bud, it's Alamo Day" (a state holiday). Frantic appeals to higher authority finally resolved this impasse, but with little time to spare.

Meanwhile, the circulation manager had slipped in his hotel room shower and wound up in the hospital with multiple fractures. Bob Bottorff, my right-hand man, had been summoned back to San Francisco on urgent personal business. To top things off, I discovered that the newly hired advertising production manager had never laid out a newspaper, let alone a *Wall Street*

Journal with its then unique and unorthodox six-column format. So Farrell and I became instant ad layout experts.

But the afternoon of D day a pressman came to the office area to report I was wanted on "the" phone. I trotted the good half block to the rear of the production area and found it was Bob Feemster calling from New York.

"I'm sending you help," he reported cheerily, "a public relations man from BBD&O [the *Journal's* advertising agency]. He's flying down to handle the publicity."

"Just what I needed," I replied ungraciously, and hung up.

But we did get to press, only an hour and a half late. Stanley Marcus, head of the famed Neiman-Marcus Dallas department store, pressed the starter button. I called Barney Kilgore to report we had made it, and Farrell and I went off to a very late but celebratory dinner. The waiter stumbled and showered us with Gulf shrimp and red cocktail sauce, but we thoroughly enjoyed ourselves and the small miracle we had just witnessed.

The next morning we discovered that the entire shipment of *Journals* destined for Denver and the Mountain States area had never left the ground. Braniff had suddenly changed its schedule and permanently canceled the flight.

That first edition carried more advertising and had a larger readership than the Southwest Edition was to enjoy for some years to come. Now flourishing, this regional printing struggled along for a number of years as a chronic poor relation. Readers familiar with the ad-fat Eastern Edition could not be persuaded they weren't being shortchanged on news content. Droves of subscribers who had been transferred to the Dallas edition demanded that they be shifted back to the New York printing, despite the delayed delivery. Advertising originating in the Southwest was minimal. The crushing blow: Neiman-Marcus, our biggest account, canceled its entire schedule, but not, however, before it had engineered an effort to print a page ad for premium coffee which was supposed to give off a tantalizing coffee aroma. Gallons of concentrated coffee essence were mixed with the ink supply for the page in question. There is no doubt the page smelled, and so did the whole press area, for many days thereafter. The aroma, however, was far from enticing.

Within a remarkably short time the Dallas operation settled into a more orderly routine. Farrell showed an affinity for production management, and the news side was functioning well.

I returned to New York and promptly came down with the mumps at the age of 40, a legacy from our 3-year-old daughter, Judy.

One May evening in 1950, the phone was ringing as I walked into the house. "It's for you," my wife called. A neighbor and close friend, Hollis K. Thayer, a partner in the brokerage firm of Dominick and Dominick, was calling.

"Come on over for a drink."

"Sure," I replied. "Fanny and I will be there in about ten minutes."

"Fanny isn't invited. I've told Florence (his wife) to get lost. I want to talk business."

His business: Would Dow Jones be interested in purchasing the *New York Journal of Commerce* and the *Chicago Journal of Commerce* from the Ridder Publishing Company? The Dominick firm had been engaged to dig up a buyer. My friend had zeroed in on Dow Jones as a likely prospect.

My first question was whether it was an all-or-none package. I thought Dow Jones might have an interest in the Chicago paper, but the *New York Journal of Commerce* was too specialized a trade publication to be marriageable with *The Wall Street Journal*. He replied that he thought the Ridders would consider such an offer, and I said I would check with Barney Kilgore and call him in the morning.

Barney, reached by phone at his Princeton home, was enthusiastic. He agreed we had no interest in the New York publication but Chicago would be highly desirable. At that time the *Journal* was selling about 25,000 copies a day in the Midwest, most of them shipped by air at a very high cost per copy. The *Chicago Journal of Commerce* had a circulation of about 35,000, heavily concentrated in the Chicago metropolitan area but with scattered subscribers in Ohio, Michigan, Indiana, Wisconsin, and Minnesota.

The only practical alternative to buying the *Journal of Commerce* was to build a *Wall Street Journal* plant in the Midwest and challenge a well-entrenched regional business paper on its home grounds. Naively, in our enthusiasm, neither Kilgore nor I ever gave a thought to possible antitrust implications.

But luck was with us, as was forcibly brought home to me some two years later. In 1953 the *Journal* opened a printing plant in Washington, D.C. Among the guests at a celebratory cocktail party was Attorney General Thurman Arnold.

"This," remarked Arnold to me, "is the way you should expand. You know, don't you, that you got away with murder in Chicago? Some of your friends in the publishing industry there have recently pointed it out to me."

He added: "It's too late to do anything about it now. I'm not very good at unscrambling omelets. But don't do it again."

It was not difficult to make an informed guess as to the identity of our Chicago publishing "friends." The rapid growth of the *Journal's* Midwest Edition—between 1951 and 1956, its daily circulation more than tripled, from 42,000 to 131,000—had coincided with an equally steady drop in *Chicago Tribune* circulation, particularly in the hinterland. Whether this was cause and effect is doubtful, but *Tribune* executives of that era made no secret of their enmity toward the *Journal.*

So, in December 1950, after months of tedious negotiations, I presented the final deal to the Dow Jones board of directors, Kilgore having been laid by the heels by a virulent flu bug. We would buy the assets of the *Chicago Journal of Commerce* for $1,500,000. This included the newsprint contracts, a point on which the whole arrangement came close to foundering. The United States was fighting in Korea. Newsprint was in extremely short supply; the so-called spot (noncontract) market price had risen to astronomical heights, and there wasn't much to be had at any price. I finally told the Ridder negotiators: "No newsprint contract, no deal." I was speaking the literal truth. We had to have the paper to continue publication in Chicago.

Today, with the publishing chains scrambling to pay $15 million or more for smaller community newspapers, the price happily accepted by the Ridders for their Chicago property seems minuscule. But it was big money to Dow Jones and big money to the Ridders, who promptly took it and bought the San Jose, California, newspaper, a property on which they have made a fortune.

But, as I explained to our directors, Dow Jones was buying more than a newspaper. It was buying the Midwest franchise and a clear field nationally.

A true Bostonian, Laurie Lombard grumbled that "capital is hard to come by." But, as usual, he came down on the side of the angels and supported the expenditure.

A few days later, armed with the board's resolution and a check for $1,500,000 signed by Barney Kilgore (the only company check he signed in his entire career), I attended the closing and signed the contracts on behalf of Dow Jones.

As I was leaving my office, I found Henry Grimes waiting around the corner.

"Bill," he said, "I want you to stop by the newsroom on your way out. Those people are all your friends. Many you hired. You know their wives and their children. Then think to yourself, 'I'm on my way to ruin Dow Jones and put all these people out of work.' "

With the fresh memory of the horrendous financial problems created by the launching of the *Journal's* Pacific Coast Edition in 1929, Grimes was dead set against any type of geographic expansion. He had been extremely wary about the earlier establishment of the Southwest Edition. He was convinced the Chicago acquisition could bring nothing but disaster.

"There's a war on. Newsprint is in short supply. This is the worst time to expand."

It was in an argument with Grimes that Barney Kilgore coined one of his axioms: "There never is a good time to do anything. So you do it when you have a chance."

Dow Jones' invasion of Chicago was far different from the chaotic start-up of the Southwest Edition. Top executives gathered in Chicago along with Bob Bottorff, who had been transferred from the Pacific Coast Edition to head up the new Midwest operation. Feemster was there to reorganize advertising sales, Joe Ackell to handle production, and McCormack and I on the news side.

Official takeover day was January 1, 1951. We gave ourselves a New Year's Eve party at the Drake Hotel, which adjourned, by prior unanimous agreement, at the stroke of midnight. The only employee of the *Chicago Journal of Commerce* present was Al Shuman, the production manager. We were sure of both his ability and his loyalty.

The morning of January 1, the Dow Jones group descended on the decrepit Grand Street plant of the *Journal of Commerce*. I carried the new page one logotype, which proclaimed that the newspaper about to be published was "The Chicago Journal of Commerce Edition of The Wall Street Journal." One of our fears was that the Chicago business community would deeply resent the disappearance of its local business publication.

The January 2 edition, and the editions which followed for several weeks, were printed in the old eight-column format. Eventually both format and name were altered to conform with the other printings of the *Journal,* and the *Journal of Commerce* became the Midwest Edition of *The Wall Street Journal.*

The plant and staff were full of surprises, a few pleasant but most decidedly unpleasant. We discovered newsmen who sold advertising; accounts receivable which didn't exist, a particularly unpleasant surprise to the Ridder Company, which had, as customary, guaranteed them; "editors" galore and mighty few reporters. Pay scales, except in the mechanical departments, were subnormal. The Newspaper Guild, for obvious reasons, had recently won a representation election, and negotiations were imminent.

I had been warned the production facilities were "obsolescent." This proved to be an optimistic exaggeration.

The press was a genuine antique. Al Shuman had been coaxing it into reluctant operation by devoted nursing and ingenious in-house repairs. If ever a piece of machinery deserved the description "held together by baling wire," it was that *Journal of Commerce* press. The composing room was the most disorganized-looking operation I had ever seen. I asked Shuman why the typesetting machines were set helter-skelter all over the place instead of in orderly rows. "Simple," said Al. "They have to rest on floor beams; otherwise they'd fall into the basement." Copy for the composing room was delivered by the law of gravity. It was dropped through a hole in the floor onto the desk of the foreman.

Within a week of takeover we agreed it was time to clean out the news staff.

I told Bottorff: "Bob, you have to live here. Mac and I will go through the newsroom this morning. This afternoon, give a 10 percent raise in pay to anyone still sitting at a desk."

We arranged liberal severance payments for departing members of the staff and tried to be as tactful as possible. One who did remain was a talented young reporter by the name of Ray Vicker, a name now well known to readers of *The Wall Street Journal* as an outstanding correspondent. He was one of our few pleasant surprises.

The Guild negotiations loomed. I decided to handle them myself. Chief negotiator for the union was a vice president by the name of Edward Marciniak who had a local reputation as a fire-eater.

Marciniak presented his salary demands. They called for substantial improvement in pay but still were far below the minimums Dow Jones was paying in other cities.

"Ed," I replied (first names are an unwritten requirement in union negotiations) "I reject your proposal completely."

Redfaced, he started to protest.

I broke in. "Let me finish. I reject them because they are far too low on salaries. Dow Jones doesn't want its Chicago employees to be second-class citizens. I suggest the following." And I passed him a copy of salary scales I had worked out the night before.

"We have a contract," said Marciniak.

The whole negotiation took less than five minutes.

Ed Marciniak was an honest and tough-minded negotiator, but for all the years he and I argued over contracts, we did so in an atmosphere of mutual respect.

Let it be noted that, despite his ability and skill at improvising, there was one production problem which Al Shuman never solved so long as the Chicago printing plant remained at the old Grand Street location. Our next-door neighbor was a cheap Chicago hotel, much used by hookers. If the windows had shades, they were seldom, if ever, used. It was the custom to station a printer's apprentice at a handy observation point. When activity began in any of the rooms viewable from our plant's windows, his "Come and see it" echoed throughout the composing room. Printers would abandon typesetting machines, proofreaders their desks, and all would rush to offices whose windows had the desired view. No matter that one of the offices was the editor's sanctum. "It's a condition of employment sanctioned by custom," one veteran printer assured me.

End of an Era

THROUGHOUT his career Barney Kilgore held a deep sentimental attachment for the Pacific Coast Edition (now the Western
Edition) of *The Wall Street Journal* and the staff who had
manned it in the early years when it was fighting for its life. He
had shared the repeated pay cuts of the 1930s, the "Scotch weeks"
of enforced vacation without pay; had helped invent the ingenious devices used to produce a semblance of a newspaper with
almost nonexistent news resources. He had held his breath, with
the rest of the staff, when Carl Miller, the local publisher, hurried
east to talk Casey Hogate out of a decision to suspend publication.

With incredible timing, the Pacific Coast Edition had been
launched in 1929, just in time to record the great stock market
crash. Its actual paid circulation in the deep depression years
probably was never more than a few hundred. Once you had
subscribed, willy-nilly you stayed a subscriber, pay or not. It
eked out a hand-to-mouth existence by printing numerous
"special editions," so-called news content keyed to advertising.
Years later, Bob Bottorff, who succeeded Kilgore as managing
editor, recalled personally writing every word of an "Alaska
special". He had never been closer to Alaska than Portland,
Oregon, but an *Encyclopaedia Britannica* in the San Francisco
public library was his source for 15 columns of articles about the
then territory.

Publishing headquarters in San Francisco were housed in an
elderly building on Bush Street, a onetime Barbary Coast bordello
called the Pink Poodle. Into the late 40s the pressroom, which
housed an ancient flatbed press, was still decorated with the
fading murals of Pink Poodle days, somewhat reminiscent in

theme, if not in artistic merit, of the famed wall paintings of Pompeii.

The newsroom was linked to New York by a single cranky telegraph line, which operated spasmodically for a couple of hours in the early evening after the Dow Jones News Service closed up shop for the day. As a result, most material from the parent New York edition of the *Journal* was transmitted by mail. The two printings bore only a faint family resemblance to each other, the Western version always giving top preference to the Pacific Coast corporate news.

As far as Kilgore was concerned, any PCE veteran was assured of a job with Dow Jones. This paternal attitude covered the range from Carl Miller, who wound up with the resounding title of executive director, to Ike Ikeworth, an aged printer who was still manning a linotype machine during World War II, although collecting a Spanish-American War veteran's pension.

Miller, who had been president and publisher of the Pacific Coast Edition when it was a subsidiary company (Dow Jones, Ltd.), was a continuing self-created problem for Barney. When Kilgore reorganized the corporate setup, Carl was left with no operating functions. But Barney very much wanted Miller to stay with Dow Jones, so he saw to it that Miller had a comfortable salary and a suite of offices in our Los Angeles building. The somewhat apologetic theory, nursed by Kilgore, was that Miller's high-level contacts in the West Coast business establishment were invaluable in both public relations and advertising sales. There is no question Carl had the contacts, and I am sure they had a real value. But his vague duties left him a man without a corporate home.

First he was assigned to Bob Feemster, who was in charge of the sales departments. Bob rebelled. He flatly refused to approve Miller's expense accounts as not sales related, and protested that Miller's salary was an unjustified burden on the sales budget. Kilgore then assigned Miller to me. I promptly abdicated on the obvious grounds that he had neither editorial nor business office responsibilities. "OK," said Barney, "then I guess he works directly for me." So, up to the time of his retirement, Carl's salary, expenses, and duties were a matter solely between him and Kilgore.

But Dow Jones owes a sizable debt of gratitude to Carl Miller. A highly personable and persuasive individual, he repeatedly talked Casey Hogate into reversing a decision to close the Pacific Coast Edition. That "Western rat hole," Casey called it.

Shaky and ramshackle as it was, the PCE gave *The Wall Street Journal* a base on both coasts and the springboard from which to launch the *Journal* as a national newspaper.

The Carl Miller story had a happy ending. He made a fortune from his sideline, publishing a local newspaper in Covina. The struggling property he purchased grew fat and prosperous with the population explosion in the Los Angeles area. Ending his career with Dow Jones simultaneously with the expiration of his term as international president of Rotary, Carl eventually retired to enjoy his riches in Hawaii.

———

A booming postwar economy, coupled with the remaking of the Pacific Coast Edition into a news replica of the Eastern Edition, finally plugged the "Western rat hole." It grew steadily in circulation and advertising, and by 1949, 20 years after its shaky beginning, it was making a healthy contribution to company profits. Its circulation had risen from a few hundred paying subscribers to a respectable 22,000.

Barney Kilgore decided the moment was ripe for a big celebration and public relations push, a sort of new '49 gold rush. Miller was assigned the task, for which he was admirably suited, of organizing activities in San Francisco and Los Angeles, and rounding up the West Coast's movers and shakers. I was charged with the logistics on the New York end. A Dow Jones directors meeting was scheduled for October in San Francisco; all directors, top management people, major stockholders (Dow Jones was still a private company), and spouses were invited.

I chartered a private railroad car, stocked it with what I naively thought would be an adequate supply of liquor, and we set off for Chicago, hitched to the end of the Twentieth Century Limited. During the enforced stopover in that city (remember "Hogs can travel direct to the Pacific Coast, why can't people?"), the males visited our Chicago offices. The ladies toured the stockyards; lunched at the Stockyard Inn; and then visited the Field Museum, accompanied on this expedition by 12-year-old Jimmy Lombard, one of Director Laurie Lombard's sons.

Said young Jimmy on emerging from the museum: "I'll bet these Chicagoans are mighty proud to have us Bostonians visit their museum!"

The remark still haunts him, but it should be noted that James Lombard has grown up to be a brilliant and singularly unstuffy attorney.

I paid only a hasty visit to our Chicago offices and then went off to arrange with a liquor store to deliver an adequate replenishment for my depleted stock of potables. Also to ensure that our private car was attached, as ordered, to the City of San Francisco, departing that evening.

All went well with the logistics, and we set off, celebrating en route a three-time-zone, 26-hour birthday for Director William C. Cox, husband of Jessie Bancroft Cox. "You can't go to bed yet; it's still my birthday."

Unhappily, one director who could not make the trip was the much-loved matriarch of "the family," Mrs. Hugh Bancroft, Sr. Up to the last moment she insisted she would go, "doctors or no doctors," but her family managed to talk her out of it.

The West Coast celebrations were a great success, and we inaugurated the debut of brand-new twin flatbed presses. Joe Ackell had purchased them at a bargain from the Army as war surplus. They had been bound for Guam to publish an edition of *Stars and Stripes* when Japan surrendered.

Mrs. Bancroft's health continued to fail, and she died on December 21, 1949, in her Back Bay Boston home, deeply mourned by family, friends, and her employees. Her contributions to the company and to *The Wall Street Journal* were enormous. But they are difficult to definitively appraise for anyone who did not know this remarkable woman, because they were essentially negative. This is not to minimize her role. In essence, she was *the* owner. Thus, the things she did *not* do, the mistakes she did *not* make, set her apart from many less enlightened, less dedicated newspaper proprietors.

She regarded *The Wall Street Journal* as a sacred trust, left in her temporary safekeeping. Constantly subjected to pressures on news coverage and editorial policy, to my knowledge she never once yielded an inch or interfered in editorial operations in any way.

Her standard answer when pressed was: "You'll have to go talk to the men about that."

She well knew there really were no "men" to talk to, but it was a thoroughly disarming reply.

Once she remarked to me:

"You know, I have a very important job. I have a say in naming the president of Dow Jones, and then I leave him alone. And that's a big part of my job too."

Raised in an aura of great wealth, she was undaunted and uncomplaining when the depression and the financial problems of Dow Jones vastly eroded her income. Once, making conversation, I asked if she intended to go to Florida in the coming winter months.

"You know better," she replied with a twinkle in her eyes, "you boys have better uses for the money than paying me dividends." In the same year her financial adviser told me Mrs. Bancroft had spent more on private pensions to retired family retainers than on her own living expenses.

Mrs. Bancroft left a proud heritage of editorial independence and integrity, a legacy which has been steadfastly, even fanatically, nurtured by her heirs. It has been aptly said that a great publication mirrors the character of its ownership. Its controlling ownership has been Dow Jones' and *The Wall Street Journal's* greatest intangible asset.

Dow Jones is listed on the New York Stock Exchange, and at current prices it has a market value of some $900 million. As this is written, the Bancroft family still owns more than 50 percent of the company's stock, the major portion of this holding concentrated in the hands of Mrs. Bancroft's two daughters and the estate of their brother, the late Hugh Bancroft, Jr. Three members of "the family" sit on the company's board of directors, Jessie Bancroft Cox, Jane Bancroft Cook, and William C. Cox, Jr.

And those early investors astute enough, or daring enough, to purchase the first Dow Jones shares to be placed in public hands, have seen the stock split 90 for 1, and the current dividend based on the original unsplit stock steadily increased to $1,296 annually.

The day after Mrs. Bancroft's death, my secretary told me that Mr. Joseph Pew of Sun Oil was calling from Philadelphia.

That aged but redoubtable industrialist urgently wanted to know whether the death of Mrs. Bancroft would force her estate to sell control of Dow Jones and its *Wall Street Journal.* If so, said he, just let me know how much money the management needs to buy control and "I'll personally lend you the money."

"It's vital," he added, "to keep control of the *Journal* in good hands."

I gather he called me, rather than Barney Kilgore, because he had known me back in Liberty League days.

I assured Mr. Pew that his offer was greatly appreciated, but I was certain Mrs. Bancroft's estate was in good shape.

16

"The Standard Is Perfection"

THE old-time movie magazines habitually published a formula feature article whenever a new star emerged: "Will Success Spoil So-and-So?"

Throughout the 1950s, as *The Wall Street Journal* grew in circulation, advertising volume, prestige, and profits, a constant nagging dread was that with success would come complacency and, equally to be feared, a loss of the spirit of pioneering journalism. The editorial product must be constantly improved; there must be no end to the innovative approach.

Barney Kilgore summed up this philosophy when he said: "Always edit the *Journal* for the next 100,000 readers who haven't yet subscribed but will."

Once at a seminar at Columbia University's Graduate School of Journalism, I was asked what "standards" were set for *The Wall Street Journal.* I replied that the only possible standard was perfection: Errorless news reports, completely objective and unslanted writing, accurate and forceful headlines, superior writing techniques. I added that, quite obviously, this was a goal which never would be achieved, but any lesser standard invited disaster.

Early in my managing editorship I initiated the now-renowned "coffee klatch." Each morning the *Journal's* editors would gather around a table in my office area. Kilgore, the publisher, was also a regular, always arriving with a marked-up copy of that morning's *Journal.* First we would critique that issue; then brainstorm story ideas, possible new features, new or enlarged areas of news coverage. In the formative years of the *Journal,* I would estimate that the ideas for 19 out of 20 page one articles were the product of these sessions.

Many a good news article idea came from some highly prosaic source. The early winter rash of subway advertising of cold "remedies" produced a major story on the common cold and the role which proprietary "remedies" played in the economics of the pharmaceutical industry. In the early days of television I was driving on an elevated highway through a low-income section of Brooklyn and was impressed with the forest of antennas which had suddenly sprouted on the roofs of the apartment houses beneath. That resulted in a page one "leader" challenging the then-prevalent doctrine that TV would be an expensive toy for the well-to-do, an early published prediction that here was a new mass medium.

A colleague, grocery-shopping with his wife, noticed that there were dozens of brands of the then very new frozen foods, many offered at cut-rate prices. Result: A story which revealed not only an overcrowded market but an enormous accumulated inventory of unsold frozen foodstuffs. Within a few weeks, a score of frozen food producers went out of business, bankrupt, and a number of banks took a bath on dubious inventory loans. All because an alert reporter had spotted a situation which had escaped the notice of the financial watchdogs. The net result was a major shakeout in an industry which then regrouped and went on to make convenience foods an enormous and highly profitable business.

Our coffee klatch also tried to be alert to what we called "contra-trend" stories. When a postwar wave of strikes swept the country, we directed our news bureaus to seek out sizable companies which had a record of no labor troubles and to find out why.

There also was a conscious effort to think ahead of the news. Long before the bomb dropped on Hiroshima, *Journal* reporters were assigned the task of discovering what new products, or improvements in products, American manufacturers had put on the shelf because of wartime restrictions. Out of this effort came articles on such developments as the automated bowling alley, refrigerators which not only made ice cubes but furnished crushed ice and ice water, dehydrated foodstuffs, long-life batteries, and a dozen other "new products."

A dust-dry statistical report on population trends and demographics sparked a series of articles dealing with the future of America's great urban centers and their developing problems.

When Henry Gemmill, characterized by Barney Kilgore as "the finest newswriting talent I have ever known," succeeded McCormack as managing editor in 1950, he remarked to me that this type of job was virgin territory for him and he hoped he would get "advice and suggestions." I replied that with three former managing editors attending his coffee klatch, advice was one commodity he would never be short of. No one in the news department had any doubt then, or in all the ensuing years, that top management's first priority was the news content of the *Journal.*

The staff presented Henry with a quart jar of aspirin tablets, and he was off and winging.

In the modern history of the *Journal,* each managing editor, from Grimes through Warren Phillips to the present occupant of that key position, Larry O'Donnell, has made a distinctive contribution. Each in turn broadened and improved the news coverage. For example, I tended to stress consumer-oriented articles, national surveys of topical importance, how-to-do-it articles. McCormack was big on economic trends.

Gemmill specialized in blockbusters and propelled the paper into investigative reporting. Henry visualized *The Wall Street Journal* as the "conscience of business." Let him get the faintest sniff of a big exclusive and he'd fasten his teeth into it like a pit bull. The rest of the paper was left to get out as best it could; the managing editor had more intriguing things to do.

A historic example was the *Journal's* first exposé to achieve national recognition. One afternoon in October 1952 a routine press release was delivered to our Chicago office announcing that a group of businessmen were purchasing Howard Hughes' controlling interest in RKO Pictures. The purchasers were named and identified as "mail order executives." Chicago being headquarters for the big mail-order companies, our newsmen there were familiar with the names of any executives who might have the financial resources to engineer the purchase of a sizable motion-picture company. No one listed in the press release was known to them.

But one name did stir some faint memories in a veteran reporter, Ames Smithers. On the off chance, he called the offices of the Chicago Crime Commission, a nongovernmental organization which kept tabs on the rackets and racketeers. It seemed the individual in question was indeed well, and unfavorably, known to this watchdog organization. He was a "mail-order executive" in the sense that he had been involved in various mail-order frauds. But nothing was known about his associates.

Gemmill was alerted. He mobilized a special squad of reporters and set off in hot pursuit of the story behind the story.

The *Journal* uncovered and exposed the unsavory background of member after member of the purchasing syndicate in a series of articles, the result being that the RKO sale was aborted. The series brought the newspaper its first Sigma Delta Chi public service award, and kept me up to ungodly hours. It was my lot to talk to Howard Hughes on several occasions, and the renowned eccentric would do business only on the telephone and only between three and four in the morning.

Just prior to Gemmill's managing editorship I had purchased from the Government Printing Office the long-delayed full transcripts of closed-door hearings held by the Senate committee investigating organized crime, the so-called Kefauver Committee. These volumes detailed, many times with baffling and frustrating gaps in vital information, the tale of organized crime's penetration of legitimate American business. It also was a definitive who's who of criminals and, even more interesting to us, of prominent individuals who had felt it expedient, or perhaps safer, to play ball with racketeers.

Henry and I were particularly intrigued by the repeated mention of a prominent and ultrawealthy businessman who, time after time, seemed to be lurking on the fringes of dubious or unsavory doings. We decided to take a good hard look at his career.

Let it be said immediately that we never got any further than had the Kefauver Committee investigators. After weeks of effort we quietly dropped the project, because we just couldn't have proved our case when the inevitable libel suit was brought. However, our reporters did uncover one small nugget of negative information which had escaped the Senate investigators—a vital page from a police blotter had apparently been neatly removed.

No one at all, it seemed, had been booked on that day in that city for even the most trivial of offenses.

The subject of our interest, it soon developed, early became aware of our activities. What he didn't know was that we had dropped the investigation. This had a bearing on the RKO series. Repeatedly our newsmen would report that some unknown investigator was looking into the background of the would-be RKO purchasers. They found, for example, that their mysterious rival had been to Leavenworth Prison two days before the *Journal* reporters arrived. Soon we began getting anonymous phone tips advising us to work on this or that angle. This is not unusual in investigative reporting, but what was unusual was that these tips all proved to be valid leads.

After the series had run to its triumphant conclusion, there was a final telephone call: Mr. X hopes you appreciate the help he gave you. Mr. X was the subject of our abandoned investigation stemming from the text of the Kefauver hearings!

Still in pursuit of blockbusters, Gemmill decided to challenge the automobile industry in its most sensitive area. Automakers sought to keep their forthcoming models a deep, dark secret, revealing nothing until the models were displayed to the public with a blare of publicity trumpets. In May 1954, John Williams, the *Journal's* Detroit news bureau chief, obtained pictures of a number of new models prior to their official unveiling, and printed them in *The Wall Street Journal* along with a page one descriptive article.

General Motors, in particular, was outraged. It canceled all advertising in the *Journal* and barred *Journal* newsmen from access to GM news. Then telegrams began arriving from General Motors subsidiaries and affiliates, also canceling all advertising. More than $250,000 in annual business was lost overnight, an enormous sum for the *Journal* of those days.

I made special arrangements with the Associated Press for beefed-up GM coverage from that source. Otherwise we kept things in low key. But the word spread like wildfire. Nationwide, the press, and many public figures, rallied to the support of the *Journal*. GM had made an enormous public relations error.

In mid-June the news blackout was quietly lifted, with no quid pro quo from the *Journal*.

With this major victory, Barney Kilgore suggested to Harlow Curtice, president of General Motors, that the time had come for a peace conference. Prolonging the warfare, he said, might create deep-seated and long-lasting animosities.

Curtice immediately agreed, and a summit meeting was held in Detroit on July 7.

I am familiar only with Barney's version of the negotiations. But he reported that he had vetoed any idea of a wholesale apology.

Said Barney:

"I just told Curtice that much as we would like to be friends with General Motors and much as I hated losing all that advertising, I couldn't let anyone dictate what the *Journal* could or couldn't print. Besides that, I told him, if I did what he wanted I'd lose two of the best editors in the United States. In time I could replace the advertising, but I'd be damned if I knew where to find new editors."

The result of the Kilgore-Curtice meeting was an agreement for an exchange of letters. (The old files reveal that Barney's final version was a fourth draft.) Both letters were dated July 9; they were published in the July 12 issue of the *Journal*. Curtice disclaimed any intent on the part of GM to control or influence what a publication might or might not print. But he maintained that the corporation owned a "common-law copyright," and hence had a property right in source material which, he said, must have been used to draw a sketch of a 1955-model Chevrolet. Kilgore reemphasized the *Journal's* policy of printing anything which its editors thought might be important or interesting to its readers. He added that there need be no conflict between this policy and respect for anyone's property rights.

It should be noted that, while Barney never conceded as much, he had become convinced that the *Journal* may have been on shaky legal grounds so far as the one sketch was concerned.

In due course, General Motors resumed advertising. In September peaceful relations were cemented at a luncheon in

New York attended by General Motors executives and a number of *Journal* staff members.

This dramatic incident, and the spate of national publicity it engendered, firmly established in the public mind, including millions who never had read *The Wall Street Journal,* and presumably never would, that here was a newspaper of unshakable independence and integrity. GM had done us a priceless favor.

I like to think, indeed I am convinced, that before and after the GM incident the *Journal* has consistently tried to report things as they are and as objectively and accurately as possible. In 1968, during my term as president of Dow Jones, a magazine asked me to write an article on our news philosophy. In it I wrote in part:

The Dow Jones publications and the Dow Jones news services are operated on the simple principle of providing as accurate, objective, and balanced an account of current happenings as is possible in a fallible world.

Obviously, the editorial process involves an endless number of decisions on what and what not to print, how much on each event and how important that event may be in relation to all the other developments during a particular time span. But in exercising this editing function we attempt to keep in mind certain fundamentals:

In selecting what news to print, from among the myriad events of the times, we use our best judgment as to what we think will be important or interesting to our readers, judging those needs and interests from long experience.

We avoid trying to decide on the basis of what is proper or improper for the public to know, for this presumes a wisdom we do not possess.

We do not select, either, by whether the news is regarded as "good" or "bad" because this does not make an event more or less newsworthy.

Finally, we do not let our views of what ought to be, as expressed vigorously on our editorial page, color our reporting of the world as it in fact is.

Such a news philosophy does not always win popularity contests, but in the longer run it does win respect.

There are many honest and sincere people who from time to time will argue that this is not "responsible" journalism. But we at Dow Jones would say that any other policy is not only irresponsible but journalistically fraudulent.

Most importantly, we believe that there is no other method by which a democratic people can function and a free economy operate.

Unquestionably the proudest moment of a long journalistic career came when a Louis Harris national opinion poll conducted in August 1969 reported that *The Wall Street Journal* was the most trusted American newspaper.

17

Geniuses at Work

JOURNALISTS and others interested in the phenomena of *The Wall Street Journal* and Dow Jones' narrow escape from oblivion always seek to uncover the "inside story" of office politics and the bitter conflicts which have enlivened many an executive suite. They have come up blank and baffled. They find it hard to believe that there just weren't any such episodes.

This was not because those of us who worked closely with Barney Kilgore were a group of supernice guys who lacked human frailties. We were opinionated to the point of arrogance, felt our talents and contributions weren't fully appreciated or recognized, and were convinced we were unquestionably tops in our lines of expertise. Certainly, it is demonstrably true that every one of us could have had his pick of much better paying jobs at any time during the 50's and early 60's.

Peace reigned in the executive offices in part because Kilgore handled his assortment of prima donnas with consummate tact; in part because the work itself was so rewarding and, as *Harper's Magazine* was to write, "the sweet smell of success" permeated Dow Jones headquarters.

Once, during an episode of pillow talk, my wife asked how I would appraise myself in all candor. I replied that I was "the best damned newsman of my generation."

"What arrogance!" she commented. "Well," I said, "that's the truth, and if I don't believe it, no one else will."

Robert M. Feemster, who has been repeatedly mentioned in previous chapters, and in deservedly flattering terms, undoubtedly was a first-class merchandising man. On his side of the operation, he was as daring and successfully innovative as his editorial or production department colleagues. But Bob also was cursed with an enormous inferiority complex, and he longed to divorce himself from sales work, which he somehow regarded as degrading. Short and extremely rotund, Bob also aspired, to be a Don Juan. He could be highly insensitive, abrasive, and he was almost pathologically defensive of his own patch of corporate territory.

These personality aberrations took some turns which, if he had worked for any other boss than Barney Kilgore, or any other company than Dow Jones, would have resulted in his summary dismissal. More than once, Bob, albeit unintentionally, deeply offended large stockholders at social gatherings; he divorced his wife, a close and lifelong friend of Mary Lou Kilgore, Barney's wife, and married his secretary; he repeatedly produced unrealistic budgets which enabled him to triumphantly point to his success in exceeding sales and revenue goals. Bob even resorted to such childish ego trips as posing as the top officer of Dow Jones.

Because Bob abhorred the title of general sales manager, Barney Kilgore had bestowed on Feemster the then meaningless designation "chairman of the executive committee." There was no functioning executive committee in those days. In his journeys around the country, however, Bob conveniently shortened this appellation to "chairman of Dow Jones." Repeatedly I heard businessmen who, on introduction to Kilgore, would comment, "Oh, you are president of Dow Jones. I met your boss Bob Feemster recently." Almost invariably they would add, "Isn't he the little, fat man who wears a cowboy hat?"

Barney would reply, "Yes, Bob likes ten-gallon hats"; then smile and change the subject. To my knowledge, he never once mentioned these episodes to Feemster.

In the last two years of his career with Dow Jones, Feemster became completely absorbed with building his own image, taking long speechmaking trips, hobnobbing socially with celebrities. On the side he was running a small daily newspaper he owned in Indiana, a motel property in Florida, and real estate properties in New York City. When he officially retired at Kilgore's urgent request, Bob was given a sizable "consulting" contract. A short time later he died in Florida in the crash of a small private plane, the result of an error on the part of his motel manager, whom he had pressed into service as his private pilot. Dow Jones paid his consulting fees to his widow.

It fell to my lot to clean out Bob's abandoned office files. I found five large steel cabinets crammed with unopened mail. One letter, more than a year old, was from the Federal Trade Commission advising that antitrust charges against the Dow Jones News Service had been dropped. Kilgore and I had never known there was such an investigation!

———

Soon after Kilgore anointed me treasurer as well as executive editor, I received a note from him: "Use the enclosed only if you can't manage any other way."

The note: "When I am away, Bill Kerby is in charge. B.K."

Barney explained to me later that he had seen no sense in bruising "sensitive egos" among my fellow executives unless an urgent need arose. Incidentally, I never used my warrant of authority.

Early on in my executive career, I found that the most effective way to get something done was to convince a colleague that it really had been his idea in the first place. By far the worst method was to order something done. At best, execution was apt to be half-hearted and ineffective.

As I remarked one time to Kilgore, "I don't care who takes the credit, just so I get my way." "Just so," he replied, "I think you have graduated from executive training school with honors. But remember, once in a long, long time there will come a situation when you must rear back and say, 'Never mind the arguments. Do it just because I'm bigger than you are.' "

On another occasion, when one of Barney's top people, a notoriously short-fused individual, grossly insulted him in front of the whole executive group, Kilgore just shrugged and changed the subject. Later he remarked to me: "I'm the only one around here who can't afford to lose his temper. The man's a valuable property."

Again: "Bill, always use people for the talents they possess. Never mind their eccentricities so long as they don't get in the way of their work for the *Journal*."

Which leads logically to my good friend and colleague, now long retired, the greatly talented Joseph J. Ackell. It is no exaggeration to say that Joe was the father of newspaper automation. Nothing in his background or early training would forecast such a career for the onetime insurance adjuster and accounting office clerk. But, somehow, long before I arrived on the Dow Jones scene in New York, Ackell drifted from the business office into the factory end of the business—newspaper production and the manufacture and servicing of Dow Jones News Service teleprinters and other equipment. From there it was a natural step to research and development.

His first triumph was to perfect and produce a teleprinter (the broad-page ticker) which would operate at the then standard top speed of 60 words a minute. This equipment replaced the obsolete 30-word-a-minute ticker which Dow Jones had been using.

Ackell went on from there to produce in our own shops automatic mailing machines to wrap and address newspapers; tape-fed equipment to make mailing address plates; and, most important, remote control electronic typesetters. He also modified standard linecasting machines to vastly increase their production speed.

When the *Journal* pioneered in the facsimile transmission of pages from a mother plant to a remote location, Joe again engineered a major rebuilding of standard equipment to obtain the high resolution required for clear reproduction of statistical matter. He also perfected the transmission system which made possible a nationwide Dow Jones News Service, and during the postwar period, when manufacturers such as IBM were quoting two- and three-year delivery delays, Joe invented, and our shops built, the accounting machines desperately needed to efficiently handle the *Journal's* burgeoning subscription circulation.

Joe was almost obsessively secretive; he loved to wave his magic wand and, seemingly overnight, produce some mechanical marvel. He also was a loner, and, inevitably, an inefficient administrator. It was not until Dow Jones purchased the *Chicago Journal of Commerce* in 1951 that Ackell hired his first technically competent production man, Ben Stewart, who had a sound background in all phases of newspaper manufacturing. Joe liked working with Ben, but he never hired anyone else of any stature.

I liked Joe personally, and I genuinely admired his undoubted talent. In turn, Joe seemed comfortable with me and often let me in on his secrets about work in progress. This was something he was loath to do even with Barney Kilgore. Particularly in the later years of Joe's service, I was the channel through which much of the information on Joe's projects reached Kilgore.

But a rapidly growing company desperately needed a production organization. There was no way Ackell's little cadre of people could handle a nationwide network of printing centers and oversee the servicing of a massive circulation. So, one after another, Joe's responsibilities were shifted to other executives, until he was left basically with only research and development and related functions.

Buren McCormack inherited many of Ackell's responsibilities. It was Mac who organized and recruited a production staff, using the same recruitment techniques which had served the news department so well. He scouted college campuses for bright young people, this time with some engineering or technical background, who were interested in publication work as a career. He drafted Maurice L. Farrell from the news department to be his first national production manager. As the pioneering editor of the Southwest Edition, Farrell had learned the production end of the business the hard way because there was no one else to handle the job in the early days in Dallas. He also teamed up with me to make the circuit of our plants and convince our universally skeptical employees that Ackell's Electro-Typesetter system (automated typesetting) wasn't a threat to their jobs and would, indeed, result in a much improved *Wall Street Journal* if they would just operate the system in accordance with our instructions.

McCormack also computerized circulation accounting and record keeping and presided over yet another recruitment program designed to attract bright young people to that vital, but unromantic, side of the publishing business.

When Mac was managing editor of the *Journal,* someone on the news staff nicknamed him "the nitpicker." Certainly, bad grammar, inexact language, and improper punctuation were among Mac's bêtes noires. He was equally a perfectionist in demanding speedy and efficient service for subscribers. An invaluable legacy from Mac's regime is a circulation system which effects very speedy changes of address and rapid starts of new subscriptions. One of the most frequently heard comments from readers: "The

Journal changes my address in a week or less. Why does it take other publications months?"

Mac's able department head was the then very young Robert Wilson, still active as circulation service manager. Bob, one of the company's bright young accountants in the early days of the Kilgore revolution, was drafted to take over and reorganize an operation as ill adapted to handle massive circulations as the production department had been to operate a nationwide network of printing centers.

The logistics of his task are mind-boggling. Every weekday, more than 2 million copies of the *Wall Street Journal* must be printed; the overwhelming majority of them must be individually addressed; then they must be distributed by the fastest means available. The objective is to reach readers all over the United States on the day of the publication date. This effort is 98 percent successful. The collapse of the passenger railroad system necessitated the organization of an elaborate network of truck routes, supplemented by air cargo dispatches to the more distant points. Because timely delivery is of the essence, copies of the *Journal* cannot just be dumped into post offices of cities with publishing plants, but are transported by *Journal* or contract carriers to many thousands of distribution points, either local and branch post offices or, increasingly, the newspaper's own distribution depots, from which it is hand-delivered to subscribers by an army of carriers. In addition, thousands of news dealers and vending machines must be supplied on an equally timely basis. *The Wall Street Journal* today is sold on more newsstands than any other newspaper in the world. I have bought it in a rural motel deep in the Vermont hills, in Frankfurt, in Tokyo, in airports, supermarkets, drugstores, and hotels all over the United States.

This enormously complex distribution system is guided by Wilson's circulation service department, whose head-quarters are in a building in Chicopee, Massachusetts, quite appropriately dedicated to Buren McCormack.

As Dow Jones grew and demanded more general executive talent, McCormack relinquished his operating responsibilities to yet another draftee from the accounting department, John J. McCarthy, Farrell's successor as national production manager. McCormack became vice president and eventually executive vice president. But, like Bob Feemster and Joe Ackell, he became an unhappy man. Like Feemster, he felt that somehow his contribution had not been properly recognized. Aware of the problem, and fully sharing my fondness for Mac, Barney Kilgore stepped in with a series of ego-flattering actions. Thus it was that McCormack became the first Dow Jones executive (long before Kilgore himself) to have a chauffeur-driven company car. Kilgore delegated Mac to serve as Dow Jones representative to various professional organizations and substantially eliminated the salary gap between the two of us. In March 1965, on his recommendation, the board voted to elect both of us directors.

When I succeeded a terminally ill Kilgore in 1966, McCormack was elected executive vice president. I also created a working executive committee of directors and suggested that Mac be named its chairman. In his last few years of service Mac was battling ill health, but in my early years as chief executive officer he was a tower of strength. In all the 30-odd years we worked together, I never knew him to give less than 100 percent to any assignment.

18

Dow Jones Must Diversify

IN 1962 Barney Kilgore, despite the reservations of some of his executives and with, at best, lukewarm support from his board of directors, founded the *National Observer*, a newsweekly in newspaper format edited from headquarters in Washington, D.C. It was designed as a low-budget, mass circulation publication with mainly newsstand sales. Barney thought he had found a void in the publishing spectrum, that is, a news-oriented publication aimed at younger Americans of the television generation who had never formed the daily newspaper habit.

Bob Feemster bluntly warned that such a journal would lack appeal to advertisers—"no defined audience." He all but washed his hands of the whole project. Bob Bottorff, then recently promoted to a top executive position, urged that instead Dow Jones launch a magazine devoted to the interests of professional women and women with above-average financial responsibilities. "Women own more stocks and bonds than men, and they are increasingly moving into business and the professions."

I took the occasion to renew my oft-urged plea that Dow Jones employ its by then sizable financial resources to acquire a group of medium-size daily newspapers, though not necessarily as an alternative to the *Observer*.

McCormack was a wholehearted *Observer* advocate, but he also supported the idea of acquiring community newspapers.

It was at about this time that Dow Jones turned down a chance to purchase the somewhat anemic *Newsweek* magazine, which was quickly snapped up by the Washington Post Company. Kilgore's reasoning: Such an acquisition would divert too much talent from *The Wall Street Journal.* On the other hand, his modest experiment with a national weekly newspaper would not. So *Newsweek* was rejected. I fully concurred in this decision, agreeing that *Newsweek* was an indigestible bite.

The one point all Dow Jones management was agreed on was that we were overdue for broadening the base of the company. After all, 94 percent of the company's profits were derived from *The Wall Street Journal,* a magnificent property but one highly sensitive to economic downdrafts.

So Dow Jones' first major diversification became the *National Observer.* Barney Kilgore's track record, after all, was magnificent. All hands rallied around enthusiastically, with only Bob Feemster still grumbling and dragging his feet. I suggested William Giles, an experienced *Journal* newsman, as editor, and Don Carter, former managing editor of an Atlanta daily, as managing editor. Barney flew around the country on the Dow Jones plane recruiting top news hands. That "low-budget staff" was quickly forgotten in his deeply ingrained dedication to journalistic excellence.

But McCormack, following instructions, set up a circulation service operation keyed to large-scale single-copy sales and a capacity to handle a maximum of 40,000 mail subscribers. So the seeds of chaos were sown in the circulation area. Prepublication subscriptions flooded in, but even at its peak the *Observer's* newsstand sales never exceeded 25 or 30 thousand.

From the day of its founding to the day he retired with terminal cancer, Barney devoted a preponderance of his time to the new publication. His last words to me as he lay dying in his Princeton home were: "Bill, will my baby make it?" I assured him the circulation and advertising trends were up. They were.

In the 15 years that Dow Jones stubbornly fought to make the *Observer* a viable publication, $34 million in pretax income and an incredible amount of executive time and talent were poured into it. The dilemma was that the *Observer* proved to be an enormous artistic success and attracted fanatically loyal readership. It was the type of publication readers identified with, and Kilgore's staff of journalistic stars produced a well-written, timely journal which won innumerable awards, topped by a Pulitzer Prize in 1974. In the same national opinion poll which found *The Wall Street Journal* was America's most trusted newspaper, the fledgling *Observer* wound up in a dead heat with the venerable *New York Times* for second position. But Feemster was dead right about the advertising.

Then came the 1974 depression. The well-established *Journal* took it in stride, but the fragile *Observer*, not a must-buy on anyone's advertising budget, suffered horrifying linage losses. Then circulation began to droop. The *Observer* never recovered its momentum, and in 1977 Warren Phillips, by then president and chief executive officer, issued a cease-publication order. Such was the *Observer's* journalistic repute that other publications began a bidding contest for its staff. Quite a few people who were scheduled for transfer to other Dow Jones publications opted to take glamorous outside offers. Regardless of immediate reemployment, all received generous severance payments from Dow Jones.

Although both Giles, the original and longtime editor, and Carter, the first managing editor, took on other duties at Dow Jones prior to the *Observer's* final collapse, they now occupy top jobs elsewhere in the publishing industry. Carter is vice president of Knight-Ridder. Giles is editor and vice president of the *Detroit News.* Henry Gemmill, the *Observer's* editor when it suspended publication, refused a choice of jobs with Dow Jones and opted for a second career as professor of journalism.

In the four years between the birth of the *National Observer* and my election as president coincident with Kilgore's retirement in the spring of 1966, I exercised many of the functions of chief executive officer of Dow Jones, although it was not until early in 1965 that I was elected to the board of directors. I originally was scheduled to become president at the same time, but, as Barney explained, he didn't want anyone to think he was retiring because he was too ill to carry on.

However, preoccupied with making the *Observer* a success, Barney left day-by-day operations pretty much to me. It was during my "regency," as one associate termed it, that Dow Jones was launched on the, to us, uncharted seas of international operations.

Albert Anastasia, onetime *Journal* reporter turned sales manager, first broached the idea. Returning from a trip to London, he reported that there seemed to be an eager British market for Dow Jones news. Bob Bottorff, then executive editor,

Theodore Callis, the vice president for sales, and I agreed that Al's idea was well worth exploring. But eventually we grew more ambitious. Why stop at Britain? Why not the whole foreign spectrum?

We were convinced that here was a sizable, and potentially profitable, market for information which Dow Jones was uniquely qualified to serve. World War II had unified the regional economies of the United States, and thus created the market which *The Wall Street Journal* had been adapted to serve. The explosion in advanced communications technology, the proliferation of jet air service, the rapid growth of multinational corporations and banking, plus a variety of social and economic factors, all seemed to point to the same sort of unified and interdependent world economy.

Reuters, the legendary British agency, had been in the international economic news business since the days when carrier pigeons and semaphore signals were the speediest means of communication. For many years Dow Jones and Reuters had been closely allied through a mutual news exchange arrangement. Indeed, the wholesale and profitable use which Reuters was making of news originated by Dow Jones had first triggered Anastasia's interest.

The obvious first approach was to work out some sort of arrangement with our British friends. If there was money to be made abroad on Dow Jones news, we wanted our share. There were a couple of cordial preliminary discussions with "Kim" Rogers, Reuters' North American manager. Then in March 1965, Bob Bottorff, Callis, and I met with Reuters executives, including Nelson, manager of that company's "Comtel" or commercial news division, who had flown over from London for definitive talks. Both sides appeared to be in agreement on the general outlines of a joint venture to market Dow Jones news in Europe, and it was arranged that when I was in London in early May we would work out the details.

The London meeting was brief and very much to the point.

"We have decided we do not wish to have a joint venture with Dow Jones. What will you do now?"

"I think Dow Jones will want to go ahead on its own," I replied.

Nelson contributed some discouraging remarks about the "diminishing" demand for American business and financial news and added that the Post Office could be a "problem" to deal with. (The British Post Office exercises a government monopoly in the United Kingdom on all forms of communication, including telegraph and telephone.)

I returned to my hotel room at Claridge's and sent off word to Callis that our deal with Reuters was off.

It was many months before we learned the reason for Reuters' puzzling and abrupt about-face. That company's directors had decided to explore an invasion of the American market in head-to-head competition with Dow Jones. The decision apparently had been reached in the brief interval between the New York luncheon and my London visit.

Meanwhile, by coincidence, United Press International, one of the two major US press associations, approached Dow Jones with a proposal for a joint-venture international business and financial news service. This looked promising; the UPI was far stronger in foreign markets than it was domestically. However, months of talks produced no concrete results. Warren Phillips was in charge of negotiations. He became convinced the project never would get off the ground, largely because the chronically strapped UP lacked the financial wherewithal to be a useful partner.

Phillips then approached the Associated Press, the dominant American news agency, and met with active interest. In a relatively short time he worked out an agreement to launch a 50–50 venture. Basically, the Associated Press would handle the business and sales aspects, as well as the communications network, and Dow Jones would be responsible for the news product. Thus was born AP–Dow Jones, which now supplies a variety of business news services to clients in 40 foreign countries.

Not only is this a profitable and successful venture in itself, but it has had even more significant peripheral benefits for Dow Jones.

The extensive network of AP–Dow Jones news bureaus supplements *The Wall Street Journal's* own foreign offices, with the result that the *Journal* today benefits from one of the largest and ablest of foreign news staffs. The same rich news resources also are available to the domestic Dow Jones News Service.

Equally important, AP–Dow Jones has provided Dow Jones news and sales executives with a liberal education in how to do business abroad. It is no exaggeration to say that if there had been no AP–Dow Jones, it is doubtful whether there would have been an *Asian Wall Street Journal*, or a Dow Jones involvement in the *Far Eastern Economic Review* (49 percent owned), or the highly successful Dow Jones International Marketing Services, or investments in the *South China Morning Post* of Hong Kong, the *Straits Times* of Singapore, and other foreign publications.

Our foreign operations also have been valuable in developing executive talent. Ray Shaw, first editor of AP–Dow Jones, is now president and chief operating officer of Dow Jones; Peter Kann, Pulitzer–Prize–winning foreign correspondent was the first publisher of *The Asian Wall Street Journal* and is now associate publisher of the parent newspaper.

Ray Shaw and Donald Macdonald, now vice chairman, spearheaded the early exploration of international ventures.

Macdonald was the founding father of DJIMS, Dow Jones International Marketing Services. This organization, with its far-flung network of sales personnel, provides advertising representation and merchandising expertise to *Nihon Keizai Shimbun* of Japan, *Le Monde* of Paris, *Die Welt* of West Germany, *The South China Morning Post*, *Børsen* of Copenhagen, and a clutch of other world-famous publications. It also, and this was not an incidental idea, provides the *Journal* and other Dow Jones publications with a saturate and economical worldwide sales force.

In the mid-60s, Dow Jones also began its long and, eventually, fruitful courtship of Richard D. Irwin, Inc., a successful and highly regarded publisher of college textbooks in business and the social sciences. This courtship was the direct result of a diversification report authorized by the board of directors and made by New York Securities, an investment banking firm engaged by Kilgore to study acquisition possibilities. Its report concluded that a college textbook publisher represented a desirable and compatible diversification for Dow Jones, and of such companies analyzed, Irwin was by far the most desirable if—and a very sizable if—it could be acquired.

Although there was a small over-the-counter market in Irwin shares, majority stock control of the company was firmly held by its founder, Richard Irwin, and his wife. Dow Jones' Irwin acquisition could be a textbook example of a patiently executed, friendly takeover. Here was a company which had been started from scratch by an ambitious young textbook salesman for giant McGraw-Hill. Dick Irwin likes to recall that when he made a gift of a sizable interest in the company to his wife, the Internal Revenue Service ruled that no gift taxes were owed because the Irwin stock "had no value"!

Understandably, Dick Irwin was fiercely proud of his creation and also of its independence. So Dow Jones' first cautious step was to propose a joint venture, a company which would publish and market books for business and professional men. This resulted in the 50–50-owned Dow Jones–Irwin Company.

After Irwin and his executives got to know Dow Jones and Dow Jones people, the next step was to acquire, with Dick Irwin's knowledge and consent, a stock interest, which in time was expanded to 20 percent. There was an aborted merger agreement in 1966, and it was not until 1975 that Warren Phillips finally engineered the acquisition. During the intervening years, a top Dow Jones officer had served on the Irwin board of directors, learning the business, getting to know the key Irwin personnel, helping to discourage other merger attempts, and patiently awaiting the time when the Irwin family, the company's key executives concurring, would decide that affiliation with Dow Jones would be in the best interests of all concerned. Bottorff, Royster, and then Phillips all had turns at fostering Dow Jones–Irwin relations.

I have always been guided by the precept that in a business such as publishing, where brains and expertise are the prime asset, key people in the acquired company must welcome the merger. Otherwise, you have bought nothing but a name and endless problems.

A second precept by which I was guided in taking Dow Jones along the expansion-by-acquisition route was that the most dangerous "dilution" is not dilution of per share earnings, the bugaboo of the financial analysts. It is dilution of management talent, which can be fatal to the acquiring company.

My third guiding precept was never to consider an acquisition, no matter how attractive, unless it was in a compatible area and unless Dow Jones could offer assistance which would make the acquired property a better and more prosperous operation.

Merger possibilities rejected because they violated one or more of these precepts read a bit like a blue book of the American communications industry. Among others were Dun & Bradstreet and Corinthian Broadcasting.

Then there were the deals which we would have liked to engineer but which, for one reason or another, fell through. By long odds, the most interesting "almost" was a major exchange of stock between Dow Jones and Gannett, which was to become the largest numerically of all American newspaper groups and the darling of the investment community. In 1966 it was somewhat smaller than Dow Jones.

Soon after I took over the chief executive job, I was approached by my longtime acquaintance Paul Miller, chairman of Gannett. His idea, he explained, was not to merge the two companies but to first enter into a sort of "trial marriage." The Gannett Foundation, dominant stockholder in the then privately held newspaper publishing company, would exchange 20 percent of Gannett stock for an appropriate number of Dow Jones shares. In short, Dow Jones and Gannett would become partners. If things worked out, perhaps something much larger and more permanent could be arranged later. This was Miller's proposal. At the very least, both the Gannett Foundation and Dow Jones would have achieved a mutually profitable diversification.

I welcomed the proposal with enthusiasm. It fitted in perfectly with my long-held conviction that Dow Jones should expand its base by diversifying into the field of general newspapers, most particularly papers published in small and medium-size cities. I wanted no part of metropolitan dailies and their problems.

The big hurdle, I was certain, would be the aversion of the Bancroft family to any sizable dilution of its dominant controlling stock interest in Dow Jones. I knew that the family had grudgingly yielded to the urgent advice of financial advisers and agreed to the smallish secondary stock sale which had turned Dow Jones into a public company.

I prepared a lengthy memorandum dealing first with the urgent need for diversification. I made the point, which I felt very strongly, that such a step would strengthen and protect *The Wall Street Journal*. I stressed how vulnerable any company was when 94 percent or more of its profits were derived from a single product. True, the *Journal* was riding high, but somewhere, somehow, we would be severely tested, either by our competition or by economic factors beyond our control.

I then included a thorough analysis of the Gannett company, its individual newspaper properties, and its management. Gannett scored high in all areas, as it was to demonstrate in the years ahead.

The family agreed with my arguments, and our directors unanimously and enthusiastically authorized definitive negotiations. Meanwhile, Gannett announced a sizable secondary offering and the prospectus appeared. There was not a word in it mentioning the prospective private sale of a 20 percent interest to Dow Jones. To say that all hell broke loose would be a gross understatement. For obvious reasons, Paul Miller had to call off our tentative arrangement.

After the public offering, Gannett's newly listed shares suffered a severe sinking spell on the New York Stock Exchange. Dow Jones stock was making new highs. There was a brief effort to revive the "partnership" idea, but the respective share values were too disparate.

Paul Miller eventually located a substantial bloc of Gannett stock for Dow Jones. A few years later this was sold at a very sizable profit after it had become abundantly clear that a Dow Jones–Gannett alliance wasn't in the cards.

The collapse of the Gannett stock interchange project only served to intensify the search for a compatible Dow Jones entry into the general newspaper field. I deliberately narrowed our approach by ruling out any acquisition involving big-city papers. Rightly or wrongly, I was convinced that Dow Jones wanted no part of what I regarded as the chronic problems of the inner cities and their deteriorating markets. I was strongly influenced by the plight of New York City, which intensified with each passing year as the exodus of its middle class and major corporations gathered momentum.

At the same time, I had observed with envy the burgeoning prosperity of suburban dailies such as Gannett's Westchester County group, *Newsday* on Long Island, the *Bergen* (N.J.) *Evening Record*, and even papers as distant as my friend James Ottaway's properties in Middletown, New York, and the onetime woebegone *Danbury* (Conn.) *News-Times*. As the New York City dailies fell on evil days, these papers boomed in circulation and became fat with advertising directed at refugees from the metropolis.

I also had convinced myself that my original idea of assembling a group of small and middle-size newspapers one at a time wasn't the best approach. Ideally, I wanted a high-quality, smallish chain, deep enough in management to require no transfusion of Dow Jones talent and with the know-how to become our acquisition arm for further expansion.

In the spring of 1968 I found myself with the opening I had wished for.

It started with my spur-of-the-minute phone call to Jim Ottaway, Sr., a longtime friend and golfing companion who, like me, owned a vacation home at Buck Hill Falls, in Pennsylvania's Pocono Mountains.

"Jim," said I, "you have had a lot of experience in buying newspaper properties, but you tell me you have all you can digest right now. If you hear of anything good that you aren't interested in, let me know."

No hesitation. "How about a group?" asked Jim. "How about the Ottaway papers?"

It is a picturesque and widely believed tale that we shook hands on the deal during a round of golf at Buck Hill.

The truth of the matter is that we reached agreement after many, many months of hard and at times rather acrimonious bargaining in which Jim was ably seconded by his son and heir apparent, James, Jr., and I by Warren Phillips, who by then was vice president and general manager of Dow Jones.

Both sides very much wanted the merger. The Ottaway group of eight (soon to be nine) papers fitted my prescription for the ideal acquisition candidate. The Ottaways had always put heavy emphasis on news quality and published good newspapers in small and middle-size communities. The chain was deep in management talent. The senior Ottaway had a wide acquaintance among publishers and was universally liked and respected. Given Dow Jones' financial resources, I visualized him as the man who could round up additional desirable acquisitions.

Jim, Jr., then publisher of the New Bedford paper, had grown up
in the business. I fully agreed with his father that Jimmy was his
logical successor. I had known the younger Ottaway since as a
teenager he had been my long-suffering caddy on the Buck Hill
golf course. I had cheered along with his proud parent when
Jimmy had been selected to head the Yale student newspaper;
had witnessed with admiration the improvement of the *Strouds-
burg* (Pa.) *Record* under his editorship. Later I had seen him
tested under fire when he battled, and won, a strike at New
Bedford.

The Ottaways, who had rejected out of hand other acquisition
offers, obviously liked the idea of an association with Dow Jones.
They admired our emphasis on news quality, our dedication to
and expertise in technology. Also, they were greatly intrigued
with the idea of becoming the acquisition arm of Dow Jones.

So, from the beginning, it was a matter of price. Eventually we
agreed on roundly 1 million shares of Dow Jones stock. At the
then market, this represented $36 million, or 24 times the
projected Ottaway 1970 annual earnings of $1.5 million. There
was nothing between us but a handshake.

Before a written contract could be signed, the stock market fell
out of bed, Dow Jones stock with all the rest.

The Ottaways had every excuse to at least seek a renegotiation,
but to their everlasting credit neither father nor son even mentioned their eroded purchase price.

However, in the midst of the negotiations, and before the
handshake on price, there was a remarkable episode which could
only be possible between people who thoroughly trusted each
other.

One morning, Jim, Sr., called. The newspaper in Sunbury,
Pennsylvania, had been offered to him. No auction to the highest
bidder was involved. Just did Jim want to buy?

Jim did, very much. He had been courting the Sunbury publisher for years. But Ottaway borrowing capacity had been
stretched to the limit with the recent acquisition of the New
Bedford and Cape Cod newspapers. So, asked Jim, would Dow
Jones like to be his banker and, "if the big deal doesn't go
through," partner in Sunbury?

Within a few days we reached agreement on details.

What ensued was my introduction into the complexities of buying a family-owned newspaper when the family is not all that compatible. Jim kept me advised step by tedious step.

Once he called in good-natured but genuine desperation. "What you need for these negotiations is a headshrinker, not a newspaperman."

Finally, all was set; all members of the owning family pacified.

Another call from Jim. "The old fool [Sunbury's publisher] fell out of a pear tree, and the contract signing is off indefinitely."

Somehow Jim managed to keep the halfhearted family members in line, and eventually the deed was done.

Meanwhile, I had had my problems in Dow Jones with the projected Ottaway acquisition.

Warren Phillips, alone among the company's top executives, was enthusiastic. Buren McCormack headed the active opposition. "It's too small potatoes to bother with. Why it's no bigger than *Barron's*, and they have papers in chronic poorhouses like New Bedford and Plattsburgh." Some of my other executives were, at best, in the words of an Irish cabinet minister, "neutral, but neutral against."

However, I plowed ahead following the Kilgore maxim that there comes a time when a chief executive officer says, "Do it because I'm bigger than you are." The contract was signed in July 1970.

The Ottaway group has grown to 20 dailies, thanks to the skillful negotiations of Jim Ottaway, Sr., backed by the deep pockets of the parent company. A number of the original Ottaway markets have enjoyed explosive growth. New Bedford and Plattsburgh, Mac's "chronic poorhouses," have been consistently highly profitable. Jim Jr.'s dream of a Dow Jones–assisted move into advanced technology has been realized.

In 1979 the Ottaway group's earnings of $8,270,00 were more than quintuple the $1,500,000 projected for 1970.

And my irreverent former caddy, Jim, Jr., is now chief executive officer of the Ottaway subsidiary and a corporate vice president of the parent. At a recent golf outing for Dow Jones editors, Jimmy, as usual, shot an effortless near-par round.

"How do you play such good golf," inquired an admiring defeated competitor, "when you only manage a few rounds a year?"

"It's easy," replied Jimmy. "I used to caddy for Bill here, and I just do everything the opposite of what he did."

The Promotion I Never Wanted

"I have cancer, but I am going to live my life as though I didn't."

This from Barney Kilgore to me one morning in 1965.

He added that he planned to retire as chief executive officer in the spring of the following year. He would recommend me to the board as his successor. He would be chairman of the board, but would make his office in our new building near Princeton. "You will have a clear field."

I had, of course, known he had been in the Princeton Hospital for "minor surgery." But even after his terse, matter-of-fact announcement, I found it impossible to accept the fact that this virile, energetic man, the inspired architect of the modern *Wall Street Journal* and my close friend for 35 years, was telling me he had a terminal illness.

The rest of that conversation is a blur. I do recall that he said he would have a second and more important operation in the near future and he was hopeful this would "buy him some time."

It did, but not all that much.

I was elected president and chief executive officer of Dow Jones in the spring of 1966, and Barney Kilgore died on November 14, 1967.

Whatever his inner feelings, he was outwardly cheerful and forward-looking to the end, obviously determined to "live his life," as he had vowed, as though he didn't carry within him the seeds of imminent death. We made several business trips together in the company plane. "That's one compensation for my situation," he remarked. "At least the directors have lifted that damned ban on the two of us traveling in the same airplane."

Once we flew together to St. Louis to inspect the nearby *Journal* plant in Highland, Illinois, our first to combine offset printing presses and photocomposition. Barney was fascinated, as always, with the new technology. Each of us pasted up a page for a trial run. To his intense delight, Kilgore completed his task several-minutes ahead of me. "But," said he, "you didn't do too badly for an amateur. I've done it before for the *Princeton Packet"* (one of a group of New Jersey weeklies Kilgore owned).

Later that night in our motel he remarked: "I always feel better when I'm with you. I don't even have those damned stomach pains. To hell with the doctors. I think I'll risk a bourbon old-fashioned and have fried catfish for dinner." He did both.

Our last expedition took us to California. A directors' meeting had been scheduled in our recently completed Palo Alto plant. Afterward we vacationed at Palm Springs. Barney had cautioned he was feeling a "bit tired," but once again he rallied and seemed almost like his former intensely active self.

Literally on his deathbed, Barney negotiated the purchase of a group of New Jersey weekly newspapers to add to his *Packet* chain. So to the very end he pursued his determination to live as though he had a normal life span ahead of him.

In the last months I visited him at least once a week and sometimes twice a week in the hospital and then in his home near Princeton. He was eager to talk about Dow Jones affairs, and that's what we did. Only once did he refer to his illness. "My damned hands; I can't seem to manage to type anymore."

Hundreds of tributes memorialized Barney Kilgore's death. But I like best the closing words of the editorial in *The Wall Street Journal*, written by its editor, Vermont Royster, a man who knew him very well indeed:

> "If you ask what manner of man he was, his friends can only tell you he had a touch of genius and was to the full measure a gentleman."

Barney Kilgore and I knew each other with a concentrated intimacy over a span of 35 years. Neither of us was the type to extend friendship and complete trust easily. But we were drawn to each other from our first meeting in the *Journal's* Washington office in 1933 (he had come down from New York to gather material for his editorial page column).

I soon acquired an enormous respect for his quick mind and his journalistic talents, and I had ample evidence in ensuing years to know that he reciprocated to a considerable degree. We always had good times in each other's company. I was the bartender in the select after-work martini sessions in the executive penthouse where he not only had his office but frequently slept in a foldaway bed in an outer room.

"Your martinis always taste better than mine."

He would have been horrified to know my secret. I invariably added a spoonful of water to each martini on the rocks. Very smoothing!

Before my marriage Barney was a welcome guest in my parents' home on his news-gathering excursions to Washington. For several years the Kilgores and the Kerbys had apartments in the same building in Brooklyn Heights, and pooled our wartime food-rationing coupons. It was only by a fluke that when Barney bought a home in Princeton we did not become commuters at the same time. But we were frequent guests at "Snowden," the rambling Gothic mansion which Barney acquired, and the Kilgores were regular summer visitors to our vacation home in the Poconos.

We were equally close at *The Wall Street Journal*. Barney's fertile brain sired the broad, long-term concepts. It was my task to translate them into working journalistic practice. As Barney once put it: "I started at the top (as an editor) and worked my way down to publisher." He had done very little spot-news reporting. "Seeing that the right things get reported right is your business," he would say.

In later years, when he was president and I was second in command, it was my duty to be his "no-man." His batting average on ideas was phenomenally high, but now and again his passion for perfection would outrun the bounds of the doable.

He also was fanatically loyal to oldtime associates. Sometimes he carried this to a point where it seemed he was creating problems for the company. So it was my unenviable chore to nag him into sidelining, among others, a veteran deputy comptroller whose affinity for alcohol had reduced the accounts payable to chaos.

I discovered that if a vendor's firm name began with *h* or a subsequent letter in the alphabet, the vendor stood little or no chance of ever getting paid. Each month our alcoholic employee would begin his payment routine with *a* and usually manage between visits to a neighboring bar to work his way through *g*. But that was as far as he normally managed to make it. The International Paper Company was particularly distressed after some months of this routine!

"OK," said Barney after a prolonged discussion, "but see that he has a job where he can't cause any harm. Try to make it look like a promotion so as not to hurt his feelings." This was done, and he remained on the Dow Jones payroll as long as health permitted.

More important, it became my highly distasteful task to urge the forced early retirement (with a handsome consulting contract) of a friend and close associate, Robert Feemster. The obvious fact was that Bob, although the titular chief of all sales departments, had quit working. However, it took more than two years for Barney to bring himself to recognize the inevitable, and then only after a leaderless circulation sales department had been reduced to a shambles. Fortunately for the well-being of *The Wall Street Journal*, the tide was running so strongly with us that all this cost us was heavy, unnecessary expense.

Out of this episode, however, came Barney's approval of my earlier proposal to establish a national purchasing department. This unpopular innovation I placed under the watchful eye of John J. McCarthy, a puritanical Irishman who was not only a trained accountant and attorney but had a natural affinity for scenting both good deals and shenanigans.

Earlier I emphasized Barney Kilgore's passion for perfection.

When color printing for newspapers was first introduced, an interviewer asked Barney when *The Wall Street Journal* would go to color. Replied Barney: "Just as soon as we learn to print in black and white, and I don't expect to live that long."

It was this passion for perfection, in production as well as news reporting, that impelled the *Journal* to pioneer in the use of facsimile transmission to produce the *Journal* at its then new Riverside, California, plant in 1962, and to experiment with photographic typesetting combined with offset presses at its Highland, Illinois, plant, opened in 1967.

I happily pointed out to Kilgore that both of these developments would also result in more efficient production and substantially reduced production costs. "Perhaps they will," said Barney, "but my ambition is to have the best printed newspaper in America."

Kilgore patterned his personal life on the same compulsion to be the best. He never would play bridge, for example. He just wasn't endowed with a natural bent for cards. "Hell, I play bridge all day at the office. Why go to all that work at night?"

He also avoided golf for many years, after some brief and ego-bruising early episodes.

Barney once recounted with great relish how, when he was growing up in Indiana, the Boy Scouts staged an annual birdhouse-building contest. Barney built and entered an "owlhouse." He won first prize in his category because, as he well knew, his would be the only entry.

Although Barney encouraged Dow Jones to become a public company and helped implement the process by which it did, he never really adjusted to the fact that he was accountable to stockholders he didn't know and probably wouldn't particularly like if he did know them. To my knowledge, he never granted an interview to a securities analyst in all the time he was chief executive officer.

"You talk to them. You don't mind it. But," he added, "be sure and tell them that anything worth knowing they'll read first in *The Wall Street Journal*."

Barney was quite fond of, but barely tolerated, his distinguished board of directors, which in the years of his presidency included such notables as Harold Boeschenstein, chief executive officer of Owens-Corning Fiberglas; Carl Gilbert; president of Gillette; and James White, managing partner of Scudder, Stevens and Clark, the eminent Boston investment firm.

His method was to tell them as little as possible about Dow Jones operations. "What do they know about publishing?"

Such was his prestige as the architect of the reborn and hugely profitable *Wall Street Journal* that, by and large, he got his way without question. Notably, the board sanctioned starting the *National Observer* despite the grave reservations of a number of directors. There was, however, an insistence on a deadline for moving into the black, a deadline which Kilgore cheerfully ignored.

But in his last few years as chief executive, Kilgore began running into small but repeated problems with his directors. A case in point was the construction of the handsome office and research facility near Princeton.

This site of more than 100 acres on Route 1 had been acquired at bargain basement prices by John McCarthy, and after test borings a location for the projected office building and research facility was selected. Barney visited the site; strolled to the top of the rise; and planted a stick. "Build the buildings here," he decreed.

Fervent protests from the consulting engineer and the architect fell on deaf ears.

"Nonsense," said Barney. "If you do it right you can build anywhere, and this is the site that has the view."

It did have a view, but a multitude of Kilgore-inspired change orders, unfavorable soil conditions, and drainage problems astronomically inflated the cost of construction. Repeatedly the directors were asked to vote increased appropriations. Finally they rebelled. Not another penny could Barney squeeze out of the board.

This was the deadlock I inherited when I was elected president and chief executive officer in March 1966.

"What," asked Chairman Kilgore, "are you going to do?"

"I'll get the money by telling them the exact situation."

I dispatched a detailed and careful memorandum to the directors, well in advance of the next board meeting. It stated that we had run into major drainage problems. Unless we were willing to see our magnificent new office building and research laboratory washed away, we had to spend a lot of additional money. I also pointed out, which was the truth, that the proposed drainage system would also make most of the 100-plus acres a prime construction area and easily quadruple their value.

The director who had led the historic minirevolt against a Kilgore project moved the appropriation. It passed without discussion.

Be it noted that Barney had originally proposed the final additional appropriation under the euphemistic heading "Landscaping and grounds improvement."

Rereading what I have just written, I am fearful that I have inadvertently given the impression that Barney Kilgore was an eccentric and somewhat humorless individual. As noted in another connection, I have never known an individual touched with true genius who did not have some share of eccentricity. But humorless Barney was not.

His *Wall Street Journal* articles and essays sparkled with a light touch. In conversation he was both witty and original; a great man with an anecdote, always good-humored and always truly funny. His office memos, one or two of which were quoted earlier, showed the same puckish sense of humor. Once, when under my managing editorship the *Journal* published an article which stirred up the animals, I received a bundle of indignant letters which subscribers had addressed to Kilgore.

"Please answer these," read his note, "and tell the bastards to go to hell. But don't lose the subscriptions."

And let these anecdotes close some rambling recollections of the most remarkable man and the finest journalist it ever was my privilege to know.

Up to the years of his terminal illness, Barney Kilgore kept careful track of my vacations. When one week would go by, a missive would arrive, saying, for example, "Three weeks to go. B.K." The next week and the next, a similar message. Finally, "Your loaf has come to a shut. Back to work. B.K."

In 1963 I was hospitalized with a suspected heart attack. The next morning a telegram reached me. "Take care of yourself because Mary Lou and I love you. Barney."

20

The Lonely Years at the Top

IT is an often-noted truism that the loneliest job in the world is that of chief executive officer.

Yours are the really tough decisions, the nastiest tasks, and the helpless feeling that you bear the responsibility for the acts, good or bad, wise or unwise, of thousands of employees—in Dow Jones' case, employees scattered around the globe. You are fully accountable, and properly so, for the well-being of the company's employees and their families and the prosperity of a property valued at hundreds of millions of dollars.

This is the lot of the chief executive officer of any sizable company. If the business is publishing, there is an added burden. And, in my case, there was the burden of knowing that I was the person ultimately accountable for every word printed by "America's most influential newspaper," *The Wall Street Journal.*

Because of the nature of its basic news material and the character of its audience, the *Journal* wields enormous and unique influence. This influence is not confined to securities and commodity markets. Far more important and less transitory is the effect of the *Journal's* news reports on the well-being of business enterprises of all sorts and on the reputations of their managers.

Two traps must be avoided at all costs: one is the trap of becoming in any way the apologist or "house organ" for the business community. The other, and really the more difficult to avoid, is the trap of leaning too far in the opposite direction and tending to become too critical of business, of becoming unbalanced and unfair in an effort to be fair.

The years when I was chief executive officer of Dow Jones saw the rise of so-called advocacy journalism, a polite term for slanting newswriting to fit the preconceptions of the reporter. In short, dishonest, politicized journalism. For natural reasons, this slanting tended toward the left side of the economic and political spectrum. That was because most of the bright young men and women coming out of college in the late 60's and early 70's brought with them highly liberal tendencies.

An example of this trend was a letter I received from a West Coast industrialist:

"I have no criticism of the manner in which your reporter conducted his interview with me or the resulting article. I did object to the ensuing half-hour lecture on the evils of the free enterprise system."

To the credit of the newsman in this instance, the story he produced was accurate, fair, and balanced. But it is also true that, despite continuing herculean efforts to mold the reporting staff into models of objectivity, and despite the vigilance of senior newsmen and editors, some unfortunate material saw print. I am happy to say that *The Wall Street Journal* sinned somewhat less in this regard than certain other publications, but it was not immune.

Some unfortunate newswriting, of course, resulted not from ideological zeal but from sheer lack of care and injudicious word selection. As Barney Kilgore used to lament: "Oh, those goddamned adjectives!"

Many of the worst journalistic sins were committed by young reporters in well-meant efforts to "enliven" news reports. We once had a reporter who described a company president as facing his stockholders with a "sheepish, hangdog" attitude. Later it developed the poor man had ignored his doctor to preside while suffering from an influenza-induced high fever. I am sure our copy editors have saved the *Journal* from many a libel and damage action stemming from phrases such as "verging on bankruptcy."

I knew the *Journal* had good, experienced editors. I knew that, as the news staff went through its necessary rapid expansion, the training process was as thorough as feasible. But still I would read *The Wall Street Journal* each morning with apprehension. For the first time, I sympathized with my old boss, publisher

Casey Hogate, who felt compelled to work until midnight so he could read every word the *Journal* intended to print in its next issue.

I did not follow Hogate's example. However, I did vigorously reemphasize my policy that one sure road to instant dismissal was to deliberately slant a news report. The other certain way, obviously, was to profit, directly or indirectly, from any information which results from working for Dow Jones.

This was a long-standing ethical precept, well understood by all who worked for the company. I expanded its scope by promulgating the "Caesar's wife" rule. in short, not only could no employee of the company which published the *Journal* profit from inside or advance information, but in addition to doing no evil, employees of the company were to avoid even the appearance of doing anything which could be misinterpreted.

Thus it is that no employee of Dow Jones, for example, is permitted to serve on the board of any public company. Rules on ownership of securities are, and have been, extremely strict.

In all the years I was in charge of the Dow Jones news department, neither I nor my wife ever owned any securities except those issued by an American governmental agency. This proved to be a most rewarding practice when an investigator from the Securities and Exchange Commission would quiz me on some *Wall Street Journal* news article, as happened more than once.

In the 47 years I have been associated with Dow Jones, no employee has had to be dismissed for using information acquired in news reporting for his own profit. One "resigned" for violation of the "Caesar's wife" precept. He understood when the situation was explained to him and departed without rancor. He has since demonstrated more than once his admiration and respect for Dow Jones and its publications.

Eventually I felt reasonably comfortable that the tendency toward advocacy journalism had been pretty well quashed, with the able aid and the continuing vigilance of the *Journal's* editors. The more flagrant potential offenders (without exception talented writers) became uncomfortable and with some encouragement, drifted away to other and more congenial employment.

The editorial page was never a problem. Under the able direction of Vermont Royster and his talented successors, the late Joseph Evans and Robert Bartley, it just got better and better. Roy himself wound up with a highly merited Pulitzer Prize, as did Bob Bartley.

I am often asked how closely I, as the *Journal's* publisher, watched over the editorial page. My answer: "When you are blessed with a first-class editor and one whose basic philosophy is kindred to yours, there is no need to play policeman."

Once in a long, long time, Roy Royster would ask me to look over the copy for one of his editorials, but mostly because he professed admiration for my little-used copy editor's skills. Once when I was vacationing in Florida I did get a phone call.

"The *Journal* tomorrow will advocate immediate U.S. withdrawal from Vietnam. Just thought you ought to know."

"Thanks, but what took you so long to make up your mind?"

"Okay, enjoy your golf."

It was also my job, as it was the job of Barney Kilgore before me, (most notably in the GM fracas) to support and shield the news department from high-level attack. While our editors normally are well able to fight their own battles, in rare instances a top man has to step in, mostly because the adversary won't accept any other word as final.

I dealt with several such cases. One is typical of the kind which wind up on a top executive's desk.

An economic downturn during Lyndon Johnson's administration inspired the president to decide that if the method of calculating the Dow Jones industrial stock average were appropriately changed, the stock market would give a more cheerful message to the nation. The pressure became quite intense.

All attempts by editors to explain to White House surrogates why we couldn't and wouldn't comply with the president's wishes only served to intensify the campaign.

Finally I stepped in with a flat and decisive "No!"

Incidentally, the New York Stock Exchange started its own and more broadly based Index after I proved recalcitrant.

———

I inherited Kilgore's excellent board of directors and also his executive apparatus.

Among the directors, Harold Boeschenstein ("Beck" to his innumerable friends and associates) and Laurence (Laurie) Lombard were my particular confidants. Laurie spoke for, and had the confidence of, the Bancroft family, but he also knew Dow Jones inside and out. He was devoted to the principle of news independence and integrity. And any project aimed at improving the product was certain to gain the full weight of his influential support, regardless of the cost involved. Indeed, our only substantial disagreement occurred when I added press units to increase the maximum page size of *The Wall Street Journal*.

Laurie was a convinced exponent of the Kilgore view that a compact newspaper was one of the unique assets of the *Journal*. I did not quarrel with the concept; it was a matter of degree. As we expanded the scope of *Journal* news coverage we found ourselves with fewer and fewer columns of space available for advertising. Our salesmen were verging on demoralization. They spent more time explaining to good customers why we couldn't print their advertising than they did selling. Incentive pay, a substantial part of compensation, was stagnating.

"We don't need more earnings," said Laurie. "The *Journal* is quite profitable." My reply: No enterprise could stay on dead center. The *Journal* had to grow or face up to progressive erosion. I put it somewhat more dramatically to the directors. "It's grow or die."

Beck rallied strongly to my support; Laurie grudgingly conceded defeat. So Barney's onetime "ideal newspaper size" of 32 pages became 40 and then 48. (As this is written, maximum press capacity has just been expanded to 56 pages and *The Wall Street Journal* for the first time in its history has become a two-section newspaper.)

In addition to wise business counsel and unfaltering support, Beck supplied invaluable contacts in the upper echelons of industry and government. It was Beck who rounded up vitally needed newsprint during one of our periodic supply crunches. And it was Beck who obtained a high level Treasury hearing for us when an underling in the Internal Revenue Service overturned a series of prior rulings and declared the Dow Jones News Service not a "press agency" and hence retroactively subject to excise taxes.

Beck also served as my invaluable advance man and recruiting agent when I decided we needed more outside directors. He made the initial contacts as a result of which our board was joined by, among others, J. Paul Austin of Coca Cola and William McChesney Martin, former chairman of the Federal Reserve Board.

Beck himself had been Dow Jones' first outside director, having been recruited by Laurie Lombard when the company was privately owned. Laurie also was responsible for the presence of Carl Gilbert and Jim White.

When I took over as CEO I did make some apparently mild modifications in Kilgore's executive policies.

Barney had been completely convinced that the reins of control should be lodged exclusively in the hands of individuals with a news background. He was uncomfortable, for example, about having any nonnews type regularly attending the prestigious coffee klatch, the morning get-together which had started as a method of critiquing the Journal's current issue and hatching future story ideas. It has long since become more a meeting of top management than a meeting of editors.

I let it be known that business side, production, and top sales executives were not only very welcome but should make it their duty to attend regularly. Unspectacular though this action appeared, it was some slight help in dissipating the firmly rooted idea that only newsmen were first class-citizens in Dow Jones.

Barney also had been most reluctant to anoint any but executives with a news background with either a senior officer's title or membership in the Executive Committee, a name which I changed to Management Committee. (Just before I became president, for example, I argued long and hard to win this designation for George Flynn, then a top production executive. Although Kilgore valued George's talents and was fond of him personally, I won only after I convinced Barney that George wouldn't be able to do his job properly unless he had the prestige and authority which went with a top management designation. Thus George joined McCarthy and Ted Callis as a member of the nonnews minority on the Executive Committee.)

I took steps to discard such prejudicial and morale-sapping policies as soon as I had the authority.

I did not quarrel with, indeed I am a firm supporter of, the theory that the top position in any publishing company is best handled by an executive who has a news background—i.e. knows the product and the types of men who can make it a good product. Indeed, I credit much of the success of Dow Jones and *The Wall Street Journal* to the fact that final authority has rested in the hands of individuals who were newsmen. Dow and Barron were newsmen; so were Hogate, Kilgore and I. My successor, Warren Phillips, served his time as reporter, deskman, foreign editor, chief of the Midwest Edition, managing editor, and executive editor. The president and chief operating officer, Ray Shaw, also has had broad editorial experience.

But I think the process which I started, and which has been greatly reinforced and expanded by Phillips, has largely dissipated the idea that sales, business, or production people travel second-class in the Dow Jones organization. Donald Macdonald, who spent the major part of his career in sales and merchandising, is vice chairman of the board; George Flynn is senior vice president. These are only two of a number of examples.

———

For a period just prior to Barney Kilgore's actual retirement as chief executive officer, he had nursed the understandable desire, and hope, that his health would permit him to keep the reins of top authority after he became chairman of the board. He had made a good recovery from his second and radical operation and looked forward to some years of normal health.

It was during this transitory optimistic period that he hatched an idea which was to engender the first and, I believe, only spasm of competitive sparring in the Dow Jones executive suite. It never surfaced openly. Indeed, I only learned about it many years after I had experienced what I then interpreted as a mild and quite normal reaction to a shift in top command.

Late in 1965 Barney, as was his custom, dropped by my office for our morning chat. He said he would become chairman but still be CEO. I would be given the title of president. In a few years I would become vice chairman of the board and McCormack would have a turn as president and perhaps after McCormack, Bob Bottorff. "It would be nice for all the top people before they retire to be able to say, "I was president of DJ."

Not too long after this conversation, Barney experienced a recurrence of active cancer symptoms. He never again mentioned to me his idea of a revolving presidency. In due course, Barney retired and I was named president but also CEO. What I didn't know until much later was that Barney had discussed his idea with McCormack, Bottorff and other top executives. He never did mention it to his directors.

Apparently more than one vice president held his breath for several years, waiting for the board of directors to implement the chain of succession.

What was the genesis of this unorthodox idea? Knowing Barney Kilgore as well as I did, I think I know. He regarded the presidency of Dow Jones as the pinnacle to which any newspaperman could aspire. He wanted to bestow this distinguished service decoration on all his old-time associates.

Only once in the many talks we had in his last few months did Barney bring up the subject of Dow Jones executives. "Bring Don [Donald Macdonald] along fast. He's one hell of a salesman, and he's got what it takes, brass balls." Then, "And find something important for Roy [Vermont Royster] to do. He's lazy, but he's smart as hell." Obviously, he didn't think it necessary to mention the talents of McCormack, Bottorff, or Phillips.

On another occasion he remarked:

"One of these days you may find it useful to take the chairmanship and name a president. Dow Jones is getting pretty big for a one-man show."

As these memoirs record, I followed Barney's advice.

21

Ticker Trouble

ONE problem I had inherited with the presidency of Dow Jones was to prove far more recalcitrant than the mild directors' rebellion over the Princeton building's cost overrun. The Dow Jones News Service was in deep trouble.

Measured solely by gross revenues and profits, the News Service appears to be a minor factor in the company's operations. But it is crucial to the quality of *The Wall Street Journal*. The ticker's demands for fast and accurate coverage of the whole spectrum of business and financial news are the whip and spur which keep the reporting staff functioning at peak performance.

The News Service's problems were particularly humiliating for a company which historically had taken pride in pioneering the use of the most advanced technology. The Dow Jones telegraph printer, built in our own shop to our own patent design, was in its day a marvel of simplicity and efficiency. But it had a peak delivery speed of 60 words a minute, noncompetitive with the 100- and 150-word-a-minute equipment in general use.

Seeking to adhere to the company's longtime, highly profitable policy of using printers of its own manufacture, Joe Ackell and his research people had been struggling for several years to perfect a modification which would speed up the existing basic equipment. Kilgore also had contracted with an outside electronics firm to conduct parallel research.

The outside contractor was the first to throw in the sponge. "It will take at least three more years." Ackell persisted. "Be patient," I was told. Success was just over the horizon.

When I became chief executive officer, that horizon was becoming more and more distant. And Dow Jones continued to operate its News Service with equipment which had passed from obsolescent to obsolete.

To compound our problems, Reuters, the British news agency, mounted its invasion of the U.S. market with a competing service using high-speed transmission. Its partner was a well-heeled, hard-muscled communications conglomerate, General Telephone & Electronics Corporation.

Reuters and its ally used every competitive trick in the book, including cut rates and, eventually, persistent efforts to persuade the Justice Department and/or the Federal Trade Commission that Dow Jones' historic pricing methods for its News Service violated the antitrust laws.

We fought back as best we could. We had the advantage of an established position, a good reputation, and a considerably larger and more experienced reporting staff.

It was news quality versus speed of delivery and price, but as long as we were forced to transmit our news at a slower rate than the competition, we were fighting with one hand tied behind us.

I commissioned George Flynn, who had taken over many of Ackell's duties shortly before Barney Kilgore's retirement, to find us superior telegraphic printers "at any cost." He recommended a General Electric product which had been developed for computer printouts. It could be specially modified, he reported, to News Service use, and was capable of speeds up to 300 words per minute.

The cost was high, and the impact on the earnings of the Dow Jones News Service traumatic. From enjoying a higher profit margin than *The Wall Street Journal*, the News Service plunged deep into the red, where it was to remain for a number of years.

But we became technically competitive with Reuters.

Then came the really bad news. Lower echelons of the Federal Trade Commission thought there was enough substance in Reuters antitrust complaint to warrant a thorough investigation.

The root of the matter was our pricing system, known in the publishing industry as "opportunity for use." This method has been, and still is, used by every press agency and feature service which markets its products. It simply means that the larger the customer, the higher the price for the same news report, service, feature, comic strip, or whatnot. Thus it is that a daily newspaper of 15,000 circulation can buy the same news, features, etc., as are bought by a giant such as the Los Angeles Times, but pays only a tiny fraction of the price charged a publication which counts its circulation (opportunity for use) in the hundreds of thousands.

In the case of the Dow Jones News Service, many of our clients were brokerage houses. Thus, our charges to them were roughly proportionate to the number of branch offices maintained by each firm. There was, of course, a system of discounts and a minimum price, so a large broker with 100 offices did not pay 100 times as much as a broker with a single office.

Reuters argued, and the Federal Trade Commission investigators agreed, that this was a system which tended to freeze competition out of the brokerage house market by requiring clients to pay some fee for all of their offices even though the Dow Jones service was not physically delivered to every branch. In vain we cited statistics which showed that Reuters had made minimal inroads into the single-office brokerage market, where "opportunity for use" pricing had no impact. Reuters' entire competitive success had been scored among the multioffice firms subject to the effect of "opportunity for use." We also stressed other, to us, quite obvious points: That it was unrealistic to expect that a brokerage house which received Dow Jones news with a market impact would not make use of that information in servicing its customers everywhere. Indeed, it probably would be illegal to so discriminate between customers in various areas. That the Dow Jones pricing formula was identical with the pricing formula employed by other information and news services and had been in use for many, many years before Reuters invaded the American market. It was not something invented to discourage competition.

The seemingly endless investigation eventually came to a conclusion. The two young commission agents recommended that Dow Jones be found guilty as charged, and proposed what to us seemed a ruinous consent decree. We refused. Anxious weeks went by, and then Bob Potter, our longtime outside counsel, called with the glad tidings. The full commission had decided to "take no action."

From 1970 through 1975 the trend lines of *Journal* advertising and circulation continued steadily upward. The depression year of 1974 brought a mild downturn in net profits, but in the six-year span the company's earnings more than doubled, from just under $18 million to about $39 million. Our newer ventures, notably the Ottaway group of community newspapers, did well. The broader-based Dow Jones was evolving nicely.

Warren Phillips moved steadily up the management ladder. In 1972 the board enthusiastically approved my recommendation that Warren be elected president and chief operating officer. I became chairman of the board but retained the post of chief executive officer until 1975.

While Phillips had been progressively taking on more and more of the responsibilities of top management, his promotion to president relieved me of my self-imposed burden of "officer of the watch." For 12 years I had felt it mandatory to be available at all times. I worked long hours and, many times, long weeks. Vacations were carefully spaced and, necessarily I thought, foreshortened. It was not that I distrusted the ability of my associates in management, but my Scottish conscience dictated that if the ultimate responsibility was mine, then I had a duty to be on hand to exercise the ultimate authority. Otherwise I wasn't earning my keep.

But with Phillips around to mind the store, I could begin to live a more relaxed life, and feel comfortable about it.

Fanny and I long before had agreed that we much preferred the low profile to the endless, and to us usually boring, round of social-business engagements. We made a number of mandatory appearances, such as the formal dinner at the American Newspaper Publishers Association convention and the annual Gridiron Club weekend in Washington. Otherwise we operated socially in a highly selective fashion unless Dow Jones' business interests were involved.

On those occasions when we did foregather with high profilers, my wife was an outstanding success both as guest and hostess. Her Washington upbringing (in local jargon she was a "cliff dweller," i.e., native Washingtonian) endowed her with a charming lack of awe of big names or big wealth. This, combined with informal and natural friendliness, was sure to thaw any tycoon, corporate or governmental.

"If your feet are as tired as mine, why don't we kick off our shoes?" A Du Pont resplendant in white tie and tails did, and so did my wife.

At a State Department luncheon for Marshal Tito, Fanny's table companion was an iron curtain diplomat. After lunch was over, my wife reported in. "I had a wonderful time. He's a dear, friendly man. I know all about his family. He wants to educate his two sons in the United States. But, poor fellow, he does have his problems working for a communist government."

At the same luncheon, I had the good luck to wind up at the table with the Yugoslav president. I have seldom met a man with as abundant charm. His English, incidentally,was fluent and almost accentless. I complimented Tito on his command of the language. He smiled. "I should handle it well; I had a good tutor. Randolph Churchill was a liaison officer with me during the war."

However, when the time came for the usual ceremonial toasts, Marshal Tito delivered his toast in Croatian, and it was translated by a young aide standing behind him.

Later Fanny and I were thanking our host. "I'm afraid, Bill," he apologized, "that you had a difficult time with Marshal Tito. It's always tiresome conversing through an interpreter."

I replied that Tito spoke somewhat better English than I did.

"What! The old fox pretends he doesn't understand or speak a word!"

In the first year of the Nixon administration, Fanny returned from a White House dinner for newspaper wives.

"How did it go?"

"Just fine. I sat next to Pat Nixon. She's nice but terribly shy. But we had fun, and our table wound up as the noisiest in the room."

Long ago I learned to welcome being introduced as "Fanny Kerby's Bill." It is a tribute to my good fortune and perceptiveness. Introvert that I was, and despite Fanny's efforts, still am to a degree, somehow I contrived to win a woman who has been not only a fine wife and mother but an invaluable associate for 45 years.

22

Foreign Adventures

IN the 70s I had the time and the freedom to visit Dow Jones' rapidly expanding foreign outposts and help promote the company's growth in the international field.

One such expedition took me to West Germany, and came within a couple of millimeters of resulting in one of the more spectacular publishing industry combinations.

In the early 70s, with Ray Shaw and Don Macdonald doing most of the work, we began actively pursuing the possibility of European ventures. Despite the pervasive rumors, we were not then interested in a European edition of the *Journal*. But we were much intrigued by the idea of publishing local language business-oriented newspapers in Europe.

Eventually our contacts with the Axel Springer enterprises in West Germany began to look quite promising. It was agreed that Warren Phillips, Don Macdonald, Ray Shaw, and I would go to Berlin to conduct definitive negotiations.

But shortly before our scheduled departure we had an unannounced visitor in the person of a Swiss-based partner of an investment banking house.

You, he said in effect, soon will meet with Axel Springer. I am to tell you to "think big." He then characterized the ostensible purpose of our visit, a joint venture to publish a German-language business daily, as "peanuts," "icing on a big cake," and "window dressing for industrial spies."

Our mystery man departed with repeated admonitions to "think big, think real big."

He never had produced any credentials from Springer. Even his firm name was unfamiliar to me. And what he appeared to be hinting at, presumably some sort of Dow Jones-Springer combination, seemed in the realm of pure fantasy.

A few days later, on July 6, 1973, we flew into Berlin, landing at historic Tempelhof airport. At the Springer headquarters building an American flag was flying in our honor. Two top executives met us as we stepped from our car, and muscular special guards escorted us to Axel Springer's office.

The Springer building is an enormous structure, adjacent to the infamous "wall." It is not only the headquarters of his publishing empire, but it also houses the production plant and offices of his two Berlin dailies. It was built at the height of the Russian-American confrontation in Berlin to demonstrate Springer's faith in the continued existence of a free West Berlin. Springer moved his headquarters there from the safe haven of Hamburg.

The inscription on the building:

"Not in defiance but in confidence"

Axel Springer is habitually referred to in news reports as "the controversial German publisher." I have come to know the man fairly well, and I would comment that if a single-minded devotion to democracy and a loathing of the communist system make a man "controversial," then I would hope to deserve the same appellation.

There is no doubt that he has made violent enemies. I had a demonstration within my first hour in his offices. I indicated to one of his executives, German-born but an ex-officer in the American army of occupation by the name of Ernst Cramer, that a visit to the men's room was a felt need.

"I'll go with you,"

"Don't bother; just point me in the right direction."

"You don't understand," said he. "There are two locks to unfasten before Mr. Springer's private facilities can be used. There's a lock on the door, of course, but also a special lock on the new steel cubicle where the toilet is. His toilet seat was booby-trapped last week so that a man's weight would set off a bomb. It was only discovered by accident."

During the years of our acquaintanceship, two of Axel Springer's homes have been destroyed by incendiary fires. When Fanny and I visited him at his well-guarded Berlin home in 1978, he apologized for not greeting us at the open door. "They won't let me because they are scared of rifles with telescopic sights."

I was told later that he had just been promoted to the number two position on the Baader-Meinhof gang's hit list, taking the place of a recently assassinated high German official.

On that first Berlin visit we did discuss with a group of Springer executives the ostensible purpose of our visit, a joint-venture German-language business daily. Axel Springer, however, after according us a cordial welcome, departed for his northern home near Hamburg, fabled Schierensee. But first he renewed his invitation to visit him that coming weekend to "discuss matters with me in person."

The Dow Jones deputation descended on Schierensee. Books have been written about this "most beautiful of German great houses." It was purchased in a decrepit condition by Springer from the poverty-stricken noble family which had owned it since it was built. When we first saw Schierensee, it, and all the outbuildings, had been completely restored to their historic grandeur. The residence itself had been equipped with antiques of the period of original construction. Not a stick of furniture, not a piece of china or tableware, not a single rug out of period. Axel Springer had been collecting antiques for years. When his dream home was finally restored, he rounded up his treasures, which had been on loan to museums, and moved them to Schierensee.

Ernst Cramer met me at the Hamburg airport and escorted me to a limousine. When we reached the outskirts of the city, the chauffeur set out to demonstrate what an eight-cylinder Mercedes was made of. A mental conversion of kilometers per hour into miles, cross-checked with Cramer, produced the hair-raising statistic that we were cruising at 115 miles per hour, but now and again hitting 120 to pass other cars.

But when we turned off the highway, the speed dropped to a crawl. Cramer explained that in a little bit I would discover the road was criss-crossed by deep trenches. "It discourages hit-and-run attacks."

A hundred yards of bumpy progress and the wrought-iron gates of Schierensee were thrown open to admit us. At one end of a cobbled courtyard stood the great house, flanked by outbuildings with which it combined to form a hollow square. On the steps stood our host, waiting to greet us.

We were assigned quarters in the various outbuildings. All were luxurious. My quarters were a suite of living room, dining room, bath, kitchen, and bedroom.

A little later came a personally conducted tour of the main house and its art treasures, followed by cocktails and dinner. Cocktails were served in an enormous drawing room with a magnificent view of gardens and sweeping lawns. "Don't be nervous," said our host. "All the windows are bulletproof, and security is first-rate."

Up to that moment I had been somewhat nervous, but not over potential assassins. I kept wondering what would happen if anything were spilled on the magnificent Aubusson rugs which carpeted the drawing room.

The conversation was cordially routine until dinner was over. Then Springer asked me to accompany him to his study for "a talk." "Ernst," he added, "will be with us." I requested that Warren Phillips be included, and the four of us trailed off to the study. This room, Springer explained, was "quite historic." It was the scene of the negotiations which gave the north German state of Schleswig-Holstein to Denmark (later the root of a war between Prussia and Denmark) and also had served as the writing room of a visiting French queen.

"We make history here again tonight."

Then, in great detail, Springer related personal data concerning me, even to ancestral background. He followed this by displaying an intimate knowledge of Dow Jones and its controlling ownership.

Having demonstrated the depth of his research, he then sprang his idea, and Warren Phillips and I knew why we had been admonished to "think big."

It was, in effect, a proposal that Dow Jones become a minority partner in Springer's publishing empire and, in turn, Springer would become a minority partner in Dow Jones & Company.

Springer added that he very much wanted an American-German publishing alliance. "America is the hope of the world, and it is particularly the hope of Germany." He said he had considered a number of U.S. publishers but had selected Dow Jones because he felt we would be the most compatible partners. "I trust you."

Complete financial and operating data would be made available if we had any interest in his proposal. Dow Jones being a public company, similar information had been readily available to Springer.

I expressed deep appreciation for his confidence; explained I was not authorized or equipped to discuss his proposal. But, I added, I would consult with my directors immediately on our return to the United States.

Shaw and I were flown to Copenhagen in Springer's private jet, piloted "by the ace of the Luftwaffe." The ace landed on a rain-slick runway; twice we skidded in complete circles as he sought to slow the aircraft. Finally he let it run (no reverse thrust available on the twin jets) and we wound up a few yards from the Baltic. Later we had time to feel scared.

Then we waited for Phillips and Macdonald, coming on a second flight by the same plane. They arrived three hours behind schedule. Shaw and I sweated out every minute of those hours.

"I have just realized," said Shaw, well into the third hour of delay, "how very fond I am of Warren and Don."

At the first meeting of the Dow Jones board after my return to New York, the directors enthusiastically endorsed active exploration of the Springer proposal. As promised, our German friends not only opened their books but furnished detailed and highly confidential operating reports. A painstaking study of the Springer company was organized by Warren Phillips under the code name "Project Julius." For some reason, one of our group—I believe it was the irreverent Ray Shaw—had nicknamed Axel Springer "Uncle Julius." Springer's confidential aides (only

Cramer and Peter Boenisch, a former editor of *Der Bild,* the mass circulation Springer tabloid, were aware of what was brewing) were paranoid in their fear of a leak. It would, they said, "destroy everything." Even the chief operating officer of the publishing empire knew only the cover story, that is, exploration of a possible joint-venture business newspaper.

The more we studied the Springer operations, the more enthusiastic we became. At the December 1974 Dow Jones directors' meeting, the board voted to give us a free hand to negotiate a deal. "I won't give away the shop," I assured them.

The second summit meeting at Schierensee in January 1974 was far more elaborate, and the participants now included not only Cramer and Boenisch but a Herr Tamm, the chief operating officer, who had finally been clued in; Springer's son; and the Springer company's financial man, introduced, in true Germanic fashion, as "Dr. Prince Reuss." The principal contributions of the "doctor prince" were repeated references to "cousin Elizabeth" (Queen Elizabeth II).

Dinner was in the state dining room. Tamm, a burly former naval officer who spoke little or no English, sat opposite me on Springer's left, and contented himself with smiling, nodding, and winking, presumably to assure me that he favored the alliance. Halfway through dinner Springer suggested I change places at the table "to get to know my son," a most attractive young man who had been educated in England and then made a career as Germany's top professional photographer.

It rapidly became apparent that Springer had no intention of involving himself in the nitty-gritty of price negotiations. Indeed, anything involving bargaining appeared to embarrass him. He had delegated that plebian chore to Cramer and Boenisch. We did, however, have a chance to tell him that our directors had approved the idea of exchanging Dow Jones stock for a minority share in his company. This obviously pleased him, as we had suspected it might.

The negotiations were moved to nearby Hamburg. Phillips, who had formulated the Dow Jones offer, was our chief spokesman and hung tough, as did Cramer and Boenisch. Though we managed to narrow the gap, there were major differences which just couldn't be reconciled. Thus, Axel Springer's dream of an

American-German publishing alliance became another might-have-been.

There was a serious, but abortive, attempt to revive the original idea of launching a jointly owned German-language business newspaper. However, market studies conducted both by the Springer people and by Dow Jones were not favorable.

The two publishing organizations remain good friends. Dow Jones International Marketing Services provides advertising representation for *Die Welt*, Springer's prestige daily, which also is a valued client of AP–Dow Jones News Service.

Cordial social contacts continue. In the future—who knows?

Dow Jones' Asian explorations proved far more productive than its European probes, the Springer venture being only one of several which had to be aborted.

Initially our interest in the Far East was triggered by the enthusiastic reception accorded the AP–Dow Jones News Service by Japanese publications and business firms. Shortly after the service first became available, Japan was second only to the United States in the number of clients buying Dow Jones news.

My associates and I were in agreement that Southeast Asia possessed the world's most dynamic economy and one with enormous growth potential. A decision was reached to stake out a Dow Jones presence in that area.

In the course of a few years, with Don Macdonald spearheading the drive, Dow Jones had:

Concluded an alliance with the *Nihon Keizai Shimbun*, Japan's national economic newspaper.

Consolidated a close working relationship with Hong Kong's establishment, as a result of which we purchased an interest in the *Far Eastern Economic Review* (FEER), an English-language weekly business magazine, and a smaller interest in the magazine's parent, the South China Morning Post company.

Dow Jones made it clear that we were not passive investors but would be working partners. In the case of FEER (now 49 percent owned by Dow Jones), we insisted on policies unorthodox in Hong Kong. Importantly, we stipulated that for a period of two years FEER would pay no dividends. All its earnings would be ploughed back into building the publication, increasing its circulation and advertising, and enriching its editorial resources.

A Dow Jones man was placed in the key position of circulation manager; another was seconded to the news staff; and Dow Jones International Marketing Services took on the task of advertising sales throughout much of the world, notably in the United States and Europe. Circulation climbed steadily, and the growth in advertising revenues was phenomenal.

Throughout this period we continued to explore the possibility of printing an Asian edition of *The Wall Street Journal.* In September 1976, Warren Phillips launched *The Asian Wall Street Journal,* with Dow Jones holding 51 percent of the stock. *The South China Morning Post* company, the *Nihon Keizai Shimbun,* and the *Straits Times* publishing companies of Singapore and Kuala Lumpur, Malaysia, became eager minority partners. Dow Jones had established a track record in Asia.

All involved were firmly warned not to expect quick profits, again a highly unorthodox approach for Asian businessmen, be they native-born or expatriate Britons. Patient building for later sizable earnings is particularly repulsive to Hong Kong entrepreneurs. Any enterprise is expected to return an investment within, at most, five years. This undoubtedly is the legacy of long years of living with the nightmare of Chinese communist divisions overrunning a defenseless British crown colony. The same "get it while you can" philosophy is applied to dividend policy. Many Hong Kong companies habitually pay out 90 to 95 percent of their profits each year. If money is needed for expansion, you can always market stock, which is the way Dow Jones acquired its original 10 percent interest (now 16 percent) in the *South China Morning Post* company.

Our fledgling regional business daily, Asia's first, was, and is, printed on the presses of our partner, the South China Morning Post Company. The editorial offices of *The Asian Wall Street Journal* are in its building. Distribution outside Hong Kong is by air, and major markets have been found in Japan, the Philippines, Taiwan, Malaysia, Singapore, Indonesia, Korea, and Thailand. Lesser numbers of copies make their way to Australia and New Zealand, India, and the Middle East. In many of *The Asian Wall*

Street Journal's major markets, English is an established secondary language. In all of its markets, English is the language of international business and finance.

Although the advertising volume and circulation of *The Asian Wall Street Journal* increased steadily, after two years of red ink our Hong Kong partner grew restive. Warren Phillips quickly quelled the revolt with an offer to purchase its interest, an offer not accepted.

I deliberately stayed away from Hong Kong when the Asian edition was being launched (no one needed the chairman in his hair). However, in October I led a delegation to the Far East.

It was my wife Fanny who first broached the idea that it would be a great idea for the two controlling stockholders of Dow Jones to join me in visiting with the staff of our newest publication. "Show the flag. Show your interest and support."

Our group consisted of Mr. and Mrs. Cook, Mrs. Jessie Bancroft Cox, my wife, and me. Our first objective was Tokyo, reached after a brief stopover in Honolulu to recuperate from 13 hours aboard a plane. My carefully laid travel plans went awry immediately. No chauffeur-driven car; no English-speaking guide. But we were rescued by a member of the *Nihon Keizai Shimbun* staff who had been sent to greet us and somehow managed an identification among the milling mob at the Tokyo air terminal. He had taken the precaution of bringing with him his student daughter, who spoke fluent English.

Our savior produced two cabs where none had been available, and loaded our luggage, for which there was no room in the tiny taxis, into his own car. So we arrived at the Imperial Hotel in cavalcade.

Reservations were precisely as arranged; the living room of my suite was commodious enough for the entertaining which loomed.

Early the next morning, an English-speaking guide did materialize at the hotel, an earnest and personable young Japanese woman. But I discovered there is a difference in Japan between "speaking English" and understanding it. Our cicerone discoursed flawlessly so long as she was describing something on the standard tourist circuit. Otherwise, a language barrier.

But I managed to check in with the *Journal's* Tokyo news bureau, the AP–Dow Jones office, and also with our friends at the *Nihon Keizai Shimbun.* It was then that I confirmed that the wives of our Japanese guests for that evening were indeed planning to be members of the party. Associates familiar with Japanese customs had advised me that, while it was proper, as an American, to extend an invitation including spouses, Japanese ladies never ever went to social affairs held outside a private home.

On the dot of 6:00 P.M., the hour of the invitation, the Japanese delegation arrived at my suite, complete with spouses wearing gorgeous kimonos. The ladies obviously had a magnificent time, although only one spoke any English. Her husband had been stationed in Washington for several years. It was she who advised me that for the other wives this was indeed their maiden trip out. We felt properly flattered.

The hotel catered the cocktail hour, so I had thought it tactful to order at least a few bottles of liquor. Having been warned about the prices of alcoholic beverages in Japan, we were, however, equipped with ample supplies purchased at the Honolulu duty-free airport shop. These I worked in with the hotel-supplied bottles whenever I entertained. Later I discovered that I had paid the U.S. equivalent of an average of $80 a bottle for gin, bourbon, and Scotch. And that was when the yen was "cheap." We dined at the Imperial in a private room. Here I discovered my next mistake. I had ordered steak "rare." What I didn't know was that to a Japanese chef "rare" is "raw." As our friend Cookie Cook, who loved rare meat, put it in a postmortem: "They drove the steer through the kitchen but were careful not to let him get too near the stove."

It was wonderful Kobe beef, and obviously just the way our Japanese guests liked it. So perhaps it wasn't a mistake after all. The party was a great success and Mr. Ohnoki, chairman of the *Nihon Keizai Shimbun,* invited us to lunch the next day at a restaurant which he modestly described as "best in Japan, I think."

At the conclusion of a three-hour luncheon, I was inclined to agree with him; only I would have omitted any caveat.

Our Japanese hosts and their wives—they were breaking with custom with a vengeance—sat on one side of the long table, the

American guests on the other. The gentlemen were helped out of their jackets before we sat down, and, most thoughtfully, backrests were provided for the Occidentals. There were 6 waitresses for our party of 15. In addition to serving, they laughed politely when the group laughed; discreetly joined in the conversation from time to time when someone spoke in Japanese; exclaimed over the neckties and silks which were presented to us.

Every course, and there were innumerable ones, was not only superb in taste but a work of art as served. Always small portions. Hot courses we grilled ourselves, either on individual charcoal woks or on red-hot stones. I thought the grilled squid was outstanding. As a matter of fact, the only course I didn't like was the third dessert; Japanese cake which was cloyingly sweet. It must have been nine parts sugar to one part flour.

Hot sake, of course, for form's sake. But soon our hosts led a general shift to Johnny Walker Black Label Scotch. Upper-class Japanese have a thing about Black Label. They regard all other Scotches as second-rate.

Back to the Imperial for a nap, and then a party for Dow Jones' Tokyo employees and wives. At evening's end I noticed that the bourbon had found only one customer, a young Japanese reporter. Despite his protestations, I presented him with the opened bottle. I have never seen such a beatific expression on a face. No wonder. As I was to discover later, he went home with at least $60 worth of whiskey. I suspect he nipped at it sparingly for months.

The day before our departure from Tokyo, I checked with Japanese Air Lines on our reservations for Hong Kong. We were scheduled to fly out of Osaka after the weekend. A friendly and attractive clerk hammered away at the computer terminal keyboard. After what I took to be the fourth try, she obtained an answer. A broad smile. "Oh happiness, you are confirmed." "Isn't that what usually happens?" "Regrettably, it is not always so."

At checkout I ran into a dilemma and a typically Japanese solution.

My bill, fattened by entertaining, was sizable. I presented an American Express card.

"Over limit," said the cashier.

"There is no limit on my card."

"Not card limit, hotel limit. But I fix." He thereupon made out three separate bills, and I made three payments with the same credit card.

Physically Hong Kong with its magnificent harbor combines the most spectacular features of New York and San Francisco. Psychically it conveys the impression of a boundless virility long lost by both American cities.

You immediately become aware of the pervasive drive, the ambition, the spirit of enterprise and adventure, a legacy from the buccaneering Scottish merchants who founded its historic trading company of Jardine Matheson, which remains a dominant factor in the business life of the crown colony. As he was in the days when Britain's first troops landed on the island, its chief executive officer is still "The Taipan"!

Hong Kong, to the best of my knowledge, is the only spot on the globe today where the free enterprise system is allowed to really function. There are no trade restrictions, no currency controls (the Hong Kong dollar is rock-ribbed), no impediments to investment and the free flow of capital. Income taxes, both corporate and personal, are minimal. The colony has absorbed an enormous influx of people who have fled from mainland China, and by and large it has provided some sort of shelter and employment.

Hong Kong also is a place of great contrasts, the mansions of the enormously wealthy and swarming slums. But by Chinese measure, at least, the standard of living of the great majority of its millions represents an advance over the lifestyle they left behind.

And for those bold enough, intelligent enough, and blessed with good fortune, there is opportunity. The luxury apartments and mansions which crowd the mountain overlooking the city are not the exclusive habitat of expatriate Scots and Britons. They also house Chinese who have found a haven in Hong Kong and an outlet for their commercial acumen, a talent which has given their race the reputation of breeding the Orient's shrewdest traders.

One of my colleagues was seated next to a Chinese business-man at dinner. Making conversation, he mentioned having read in *The Asian Wall Street Journal* that the gentleman in question had just commissioned the building of two supertankers. "How many," he inquired, "will your fleet number after they are delivered?"

The Chinese looked at him in real or assumed puzzlement. "But who counts ships?"

My first morning in Hong Kong I was up at daybreak to visit the offices of *The Asian Wall Street Journal* during the busiest hours.

It was as though I were reliving the exhilarating days in the early 1940s when we were building the "new" *Wall Street Journal*. The same spirit of high adventure, the dedication, the heady atmosphere of creation. It pervaded the staff, from the young editor-publisher, Peter Kann, manning his first executive post, to the meticulous Chinese pressmen who treated each page of type as an ultimate expression of the printer's art.

"My big problem," said Kann, "is getting people to work decent hours. They'll kill themselves. Most of the people out there," he gestured toward the newsroom, "have been working 12- and 14-hour days for the past six weeks. They keep sneaking in behind my back."

He told this story of a young Chinese bookkeeper:

The day before, the bookkeeper had hesitantly requested "two hours for lunch, if convenient."

"Take the whole day. You have been overworking anyway."

"No, two hours plenty."

Another staff member later confided that "Chan" wanted the extra hour because he was getting married that noon and "needed honeymoon time." His bride was flying to America that same afternoon to enter the University of California.

I told Peter Kann that one of my projects while in Hong Kong was to give a party to end all parties as a sort of thank-you to the staff.

At Peter's suggestion we rented a cutter (converted from sail to power) of the type used by the British in the old days to pursue Chinese pirates. The staff, plus spouses and/or "friends," were invited for cocktails and dinner aboard while we explored Hong Kong's harbor and adjacent waters. It was a great night for all of us.

"I could work for 50 years for British or Chinese Hong Kong company and never see the chairman," remarked a Chinese clerk. "Here I have drink with him. May you and your *Journal* live a thousand years."